LIFE AFTER DEBT

THE BLUEPRINT FOR SURVIVING IN AMERICA'S CREDIT SOCIETY

by
BENJAMIN F. DOVER

D1025789

edited by
Sharon Hallberg & Linda Vanderwold

Equitable Media Services
Fort Worth, Texas

*"To sin by silence when we should protest
makes cowards out of men."*
- Ella Wheeler Wilcox

For more information, contact: David Flowers/Media Coordinator, Equitable Media Services, Post Office Box 9822, Fort Worth, Texas 76147-2822.

Library of Congress Cataloging In Publication Data

Publisher's Cataloging in Publication
(Prepared by Quality Books, Inc.)

Dover, Benjamin F.
　　　Life after debt: the blueprint for surviving in America's credit society /
　　　written by Benjamin F. Dover; edited by Sharon Hallberg & Linda
　　　Vanderwold.
　　　p. cm.
　　　Includes bibliographical references and index.
　　　ISBN 1-880-925-03-6

　　　　　1. Consumer credit—United States. 2. Credit bureaus—United States.
　　　I. Title.

HG3751.7.D68 1993　　　　　　332.743

QBI93-21205

This book is available at a special discount when ordering in bulk quantities. For more information, contact:

Equitable Media Services
ATTN: Bulk Sales Department
Post Office Box 9822
Fort Worth, TX 76147-2822

Write to Benjamin Dover at
CompuServe address 75053,3635
or on the InterNet at bendover@onramp.net.

Printed in the United States of America

10   9   8   7   6   5   4   3   2

ACKNOWLEDGEMENT

We are all products of our past. Our views and goals are molded by where we have been and dreams of where we hope to be.

So many people have played important roles in my own private journey through trial and error...so many people were there for me during my own trials and tribulations.

Thank you to all of you. I couldn't have made it without you!

Phil B.	Mary & Liberty DeVitto	Bernard M. Fife
Buck & Betty	John Watson	Stan David
Stan & Cynthia Talley	Bill & Molly	Sharon Hallberg
Scott & Wendy	S.L. Hudson	Buddy Sorrell
Homer & Julie	Karen Porter	L.G. Reese
Clint W.	Ronnie S.	Danny F.
Bobi H.	Wallace & Theodore	Mom Watson
Marshall Day	Bill & Sue Roffey	Ed & Kyle
Angelo Guiseppi	Wanda S.	Lezlie F.
Marsha Friedman	Martha Savelo	Norman H.
Dad, Mom & Jim	Larry "Bud" Melman	Linda & Stacy
Marti P.	Gil Gross	D.M.L. Roberts
Donna Wright	Kris Evans	Diane M.
Earnest Winborne	John Broude	Max and Grace
Larry Sanders	Susan Kaplow	Larry Rose
Mark Hulme	Bretta, Kent & George	Gordon V.
Joe Friday	Christian & Serge T.	Peter & Steph
Clifford Clavin	Ethan B.	Jerome Howard
Eric V.	R.A. Cruson	Paul P.
Steven Gardner	Michael G. Riley	Gerry O.
Art Zobal	A.E. Neuman	Jean N.
Ralph Marshburn	Warren Gould	

Tom Carter, Federal Trade Commission/Dallas office.
C.S. Jenkins, Director of MIS security.

Dan Bennett and the rest of the KLIF staff.

Most of all, I thank God for a second chance.

Cover design by Rishi Seth.
Back cover photo by Anthony Brisbane Smith.
Tom Parsons/Best Fares Magazine (800) 880-1234 are official travel coordinators
for B.F. Dover and staff.
American Airlines is the official air carrier for B.F. Dover and staff.
Thank you to the Hyatt Regency/DFW for peace and quiet and to Nickelodeon for
continued inspiration!
Life After Debt was written on a Compudyne 486/55 system from *CompUSA* using
WordPerfect software.

WARNING!

You **MUST** read this book at least **twice** before enacting any of the strategies or tactics that are outlined.

You are about to challenge an enormous system that is stacked against you and includes a wide range of counter-measures to defeat your attempts to modify information in your credit files.

This book will upset many people in a variety of industries across this nation.

However, if the system were not outmoded, unfair and riddled with inaccuracies and inconsistencies, this book would not be necessary.

Ask questions! Challenge the status quo in the data services community! And don't worry...with the knowledge you're about to be armed with, there really is:

Life After Debt

Benjamin F. Dover
Fort Worth, TX
August 1993

DISCLAIMER

I am not an attorney and do not give legal advice.

I am not a certified public accountant and do not give accounting or tax advice.

As with all books published in the CONSUMER/SELF HELP genre, it is important that you understand all elements of information explained in this book **before** proceeding.

This book is not designed to be a guaranteed fix of your credit bureau report(s); instead, the book provides insight into the inner-workings of the system. The author hopes that with the knowledge gained from *Life After Debt* you will be able to eliminate negative or derogatory or incorrect/invalid information from your own credit bureau report(s).

In the event you have actually earned your torn up credit report, *Life After Debt* gives you a chance to learn how the system works, explains your rights, and teaches negotiating strategies that will show you how to do the right thing to accelerate your personal financial recovery.

FOREWORD

In order to successfully put *Life After Debt* to work for you, you must be willing to invest:

TIME
PATIENCE
PERSISTENCE
<u>KNOWLEDGE</u>

I'll provide the last element but you've got to handle the first three.

1) In this book the information and the presentation originate from several areas:

a) The author's own real life experiences;

b) The author's past dealings with individuals having problems described in this book;

c) Intensive research by the author, including the interviewing of qualified individuals who are recognized experts in the credit/information selling business.

2) Some individuals spoke "on the record." Others cooperated with the understanding that their identities be concealed because of their direct association or involvement in the credit/information industries (current or past).

3) You may be told that this book is nothing more than a "CREDIT REPAIR MANUAL."

It is not.

Life After Debt presents an incisive look at the credit system currently in use and in place in the United States of America as of August, 1993.

4) You may be told I am "abusing the system."

I am not.

In fact, millions of consumers across America are sick and tired of being abused by the system. Only in the credit reporting industry do we have daily contact with a concept of **"GUILTY UNTIL PROVEN INNOCENT."**

5) Anything, repeat **ANYTHING** can be legally removed from a credit bureau report. If you have tried the conventional methodologies writing back and forth with the credit bureau trying to delete information that's not even yours, then this book is for you! Remember, it's not always the message...sometimes it's the messenger.

Restated, look at it this way:

There are a dozen ways you can ask someone to do something for you, right? *Life After Debt* will give you the knowledge, guidelines and perspective necessary to get your report cleared up promptly.

7) Big banks, department stores and other lenders will publicly dispute everything I'm about to share with you for several reasons:

a) "Company policy;"

b) "Benjamin Dover is a quick buck artist selling snake oil;"

c) "It'll never happen as he tells you in his book so pay up or we'll screw up your credit reports;"

d) "It'll never happen as he tells you in the book so pay up or we'll see you in court;"

e) All of the above.

Believe them if you wish and take this book back to wherever you bought it **now** so you can get your money back.

8) It's easy to understand why they're intimidated by my philosophies:

a) I have their number and share it with you, the consumer;

b) I show you how the system works so you won't be intimidated by their strong-arm mail and telephone techniques;

c) I take away their "hammer" and with it their ability to scare, intimidate and coerce you into doing things that are usually only in their best financial interest, **NOT YOURS.**

Some parting thoughts.....

As I have already said once before (but it warrants repeating), this book is **<u>not</u>** a credit repair manual or a blueprint on how to evade debts and responsibilities that you rightly owe.

It is a tool to teach you how the system works and to give you the knowledge and insights necessary to get back on your feet emotionally and financially.

You can't fix something unless you know what broke it. Your credit files are a series of complex and confusing reports that didn't deteriorate overnight, so don't think that you're going to fix it overnight either.

Nor can you benefit from a "simple" fix.

Nevertheless, the ultimate question is straightforward enough:

CAN IT BE FIXED?

The answer can be summed up in one word:

YES.

The methods used weren't learned from any one source or person but from **trial by fire...**and also from a substantial amount of time studying the system.

Like anything else we deal with on a daily basis in our lives, the credit system has its strong points and its weak points. When you know how to attack the weak points and how to deal with their stronger checks and balances, you will see results in your own life as you **REGAIN CONTROL.**

Will you have success 100% of the time?

No way.

But plan on attaining at least a 50% success rate (with 70-80% attainable), which is much better than you'd realize if you <u>blindly</u> tried to resuscitate your own particular situation.

People in a variety of socio-economic groups have benefitted from the knowledge you are about to gain, including truck drivers, school teachers, nurses and doctors and dentists, radio and television personalities, real estate developers and bankers...and (believe it or not) even a few attorneys.

I've seen the highs and lows of the Texas economy of the 1980's and the difficult economic times being endured by people just like you in professions as diverse as the automobile industry, oil and gas, defense contractors, and even in "stable" careers with industry giants like IBM.

<u>**Nobody**</u> is safe from the ax of unemployment or from the upheaval of an unhappy marriage, from the death of a loved one or an unexpected illness or accident.

Damn it.

We just can't seem to plan for these troubled times we're all forced to face at some point in our lives; you never know what to expect or how to react until you're forced into the middle of your own personal hell.

To those individuals who intentionally abuse the system and rip off creditors big and small and who think they are beating the system, just remember:

Your time will come.

You will be caught and I hope the system comes down on you as <u>HARD</u> as allowed by the civil and criminal laws of the land. For everybody else (and this applies to about 97% of you reading these words right now):

**THIS IS YOUR TICKET
TO REGAINING YOUR SANITY.
THIS IS YOUR TICKET
TO REGAINING SOME DIGNITY.
THIS IS YOUR CHANCE TO REBUILD A**
Life After Debt

Remember.....

> *"Tough times don't last.*
> *Tough people do."*
> *–Old Texas proverb*

Alright now. Let's go to work.

TABLE OF CONTENTS

1

THE BIG THREE: WHO ARE THESE GUYS ANYWAY?

"The man who makes
no mistakes does not usually make anything."
–Edward John Phelps

LET'S START THIS PROCESS OFF THE RIGHT WAY. You have got to know what all three of the credit bureaus are saying about you FIRST before you have any measurable impact on your reports. The *"Big Three"* include: TRW, Equifax and Trans Union.

I've been on hundreds of radio talk shows and many network television shows since early 1992. If you've heard me on the air you already know how hard I preach about obtaining a current copy of your credit bureau report (and if you're married, be sure to obtain a copy of your spouse's report as well).

I think it's important to give you an insight into who these credit bureaus are that wield so much power and influence over every American's life. Where did they come from? How long have they been doing this? Who died and left them in charge?

It's a daunting task: The "Big Three" attempt to manage over 150 million individual credit histories involving over $750 billion in consumer debt. That's three quarters of a *trillion* dollars in real numbers.

According to Equifax, consumers purchase more than 40,000 cars, 500,000 appliances and 5,000 homes daily. That adds up to over 12.5 million cars, over 156 million appliances and over 1.5 million homes a year...over 170 million inquiries on actual purchases made by Americans annually.

So you understand who you're dealing with, a quick overview is in order.....

TRW

Headquartered in Cleveland, Ohio, TRW is a diversified international conglomerate that has its hand in a number of industries, including:

- Automobile air-bag modules;
- Rack and pinion steering systems for autos;
- Satellite communications equipment;
- Earth-orbiting observation satellites;
- A variety of high-tech electronic/military applications devices;
- State of the art avionics development;
- Business credit analysis service (creators of

2

"Intelliscore," a computer program that utilizes statistical data and predicts the default potential of receivables);

* *Consumer information and services business.*

TRW has divisions operating throughout the world: Australia, Austria, Brazil, Canada, France, Germany, Italy, Japan, South Korea, Mexico, Spain and the United Kingdom, employing over 64,000 people worldwide.

TRW continues to divest itself of nonstrategic businesses to allow greater focus on its core profit-generating divisions:

* Consumer credit and marketing
* Business credit
* Image processing
* Real estate information services

TRW increased its presence in the Midwest/south back in the 1980's by purchasing Chilton, a former player in the credit reporting game, for around $600 million. Some insiders at TRW felt they overpaid for Chilton: file duplications and file errors were the main culprits, but the merger allowed TRW to have an instant marketshare...growth through acquisition, a familiar sign of things to come in corporate America in the 1980's.

Gross sales in 1992 topped $8.3 billion, but showed a $156 million loss due to restructuring and changes in accounting practices. TRW is primed to be one of the top performers in the years to come due to these actions, committing over $530 million in capital expenditures in 1992 towards their future.

Further evidence of this: in March '93 TRW purchased a 4% interest in Central Communication Bureau (CCB), the fourth largest credit reporting bureau in Japan. TRW plans on advising CCB on expanding their database to include both positive and negative consumer credit information. Until now, Japanese credit bureaus have only reported negative credit information (no news is good news, huh?).

EQUIFAX

Equifax impresses me the most with their apparent commitment to clean up their image through a heavy dose of public relations moves designed to dispel the bad image that saddles credit bureaus.

Known in the early part of the century as The Retail Credit Company, Equifax was founded in 1899 primarily as a provider of intelligence information for the financial and insurance industries. Also referred to as "CSC" or "CSC/Equifax" as a result of an agreement signed by Equifax with Computer Sciences Corporation in August 1988, this relationship was modified to a general partnership in December 1990, and required CSC's conversion to Equifax reporting formats and standards. The merger was another intelligent step for Equifax to increase its reach and become the premier information services provider around the world.

Guided from the infancy of the information age by Jeff White until his retirement last year, revenues have grown from $11 million (in 1942) to over $1 billion (in 1992).

Over 12,400 people are employed by Equifax throughout North America, the Caribbean and the United Kingdom.

Equifax prides itself as being the "Information Solution" and diversifying operations through acquisition of new but related companies such as Health Economics Corporation (HEC), a major player in the highly-competitive health care information industry.

Equifax bought a 20% stake in Transax Financial Services, Ltd. in 1992. This company provides check guarantee services throughout Ireland, Scotland, England, Wales, Australia and France. In a similar move, Equifax acquired Telecredit (founded 1961 and based in Los Angeles), an industry leader in electronic payments services to guarantee, process and facilitate the transfer of value in 1992. In layman's language, Telecredit handles check and credit card processing, debt collection services and new account verification services. This new division of Equifax is known as Equifax Check Services and Equifax Card Services.

Equifax is the recognized leader in providing the insurance industry with personal life, health, auto and property information for underwriters to draw upon. Health measurements, medical history reports, claim investigations, motor vehicle records, and automotive and property claim information through the C.L.U.E. (Comprehensive Loss Underwriting Exchange) and ADD™ (Additional Driver Discovery) add to the wealth of information Equifax collects, classifies and resells about Americans everyday.

Another Equifax subsidiary may give you a feeling that Big Brother is looking over your shoulder.

Physical Measurements, Inc. (PMI) is a subsidiary that contracts with many large health/life insurance companies to provide physical examinations and background histories on prospective policy holders. Their team of paramedics and nurses not only collect "pertinent" health information relating to your medical history, but also "lifestyle" questions.

These "lifestyle" questions ask consumers about their sexual preferences, drinking patterns, drug usage histories (past and present) and other subjects that may give interested inquisitors insight into what makes you tick, and what might make you sick.

Guess what they *don't* tell you?

What PMI fails to disclose is their *relationship* to parent company Equifax and their data bases of credit information. Combined with information already in their data files, all of the data they collect allows Equifax to sell what they refer to as "consumer reports." These consumer reports are sold to inquisitors at a premium under the old "have a legitimate need to know" cover story and are governed by the same laws as credit reports under the Fair Credit Reporting

Act (FCRA) (specifically §603(d) referring to a consumer's "personal characteristics or mode of living" and it is "used or expected to be used or collected in whole or in part for the purpose of serving as a factor in establishing the consumer's eligibility for...insurance to be used primarily for personal, family or household purposes."

Except for ONE major difference: Americans have a right to inspect their credit files under the FCRA. However, there is *no* opportunity for consumers to inspect their "consumer report" and dispute its accuracy or validity.

As alluded to later in this book, Equifax, like the other credit bureaus, utilizes statistical algorithms to develop "risk scores" (see Chapter 8, Scoring Your Credit Profile); these "risk scores" help creditors predict the chances of a consumer falling behind on payments or filing for bankruptcy. But like medical records, everyone else can see this information and these scores...except for the very people they're being reported on—the consumers.

This is a lucrative field of endeavor: Equifax reported $85.3 million in profits on gross sales of $1.13 billion in 1992. Future earnings estimates are equally optimistic as Equifax continues to diversify in the information-driven 1990's.

TRANS UNION

In the race for consumer information supremacy, Trans Union is the dark horse.

7

Based in Chicago and acquired by the Pritzker family's Marmon Group, Ltd. in 1981 for $688 million, Trans Union is the lowest-profile and probably the most stubborn of the three major credit reporting bureaus.

Since it is privately owned it's easy for Trans Union to maintain a high degree of silence. They're comfortable letting the other two publicly-traded credit reporting bureaus hire lobbyists and get beat up in the public eye from dealing with Congress and various consumer rights groups.

Trans Union claims that it controls almost one-third of the U.S. credit bureau business with detailed files on over 180 million Americans (99% of the nation's adults with credit records) and annual revenues estimated in excess of $250 million. Approximately 85% of their revenues is generated from the sale of consumer credit information to credit grantors…at about $1.50 a report.

TransMark is a Trans Union subsidiary that accounted for about 10% of the parent company's gross income; TransMark generates substantial revenues from the sales of pre-screened mailing lists to mail order companies and bank/credit card issuers. One of their growth areas was the solicitation of new business by mailing "pre-approved" credit card offers to consumers.

TransAction is the newest unit of Trans Union, established in 1990. It is designed to let credit grantors have greater interaction with Trans Union's data base in hopes of expediting credit granting decisions.

When Trans Union began competing for the credit file dollar in new market areas (such as California), their main competitors did not exactly greet them with open arms. There was and still is a mutual respect between TRW and Equifax; the quality of information and service of their clients was felt to be positive. Furthermore, spot checks of information for accuracy and timeliness indicated that for the time and technology, their data was good. However Trans Union's accuracy was not felt to be as high as that of the other two companies and this has caused some perception/credibility problems for them.

2

WHERE DID
IT ALL GO WRONG?

"In times of calamity, any rumor is believed."
–Publilius Syrus

NEGATIVE INFORMATION HAS TO ORIGINATE SOMEWHERE. The predictable reply when you've been declined credit goes something like:

"But I paid that bill!"
"That was my exhusband's responsibility!"
"The dog ate my statement that month!"

Unless you lived in Norwich, Vermont in late 1991.

Norwich could have been tagged with the "town of deadbeats" label if it were left up to TRW. It seems that one of TRW's information providers, a subcontractor from Norcross, Georgia named National Data Retrieval (NDR), somehow made the mistake of tagging all of the residents of Norwich as tax debtors.

Tax liens, judgments, bankruptcies, etc. are all accessible through public records. Since these types of files are manually entered by the courts into public record, there is a need for subcontractors like NDR. Companies such as NDR scan public records for new entries and report this information to the major credit reporting bureaus.

The major bureaus then add this information to your credit report, normally at the bottom or end of the report under the heading "PUBLIC RECORDS." Other public records that can be added include any criminal convictions (which can stay, like the credit information, for up to 7 years from the date they're entered into the public record).

Here's the punch line to the Norwich, Vermont story: one person collecting data from public records screwed up and as a result, the entire adult population that had *any* credit history on file with TRW was now listed as a tax debtor (remember, tax liens are part of the public information base). Trust me. No banker wants to loan money to anyone with a tax lien...especially if the lien is placed by an agency like the IRS, since the taxman will always get what they want, first and always.

Karen Porter, Norwich's town clerk, uncovered this miscarriage of credit justice.

Clue #1: She began receiving phone calls from bankers and prospective credit grantors wanting to know if "county" tax liens had been paid off or satisfied. Calls about taxes and liens are standard fare for her office since it handles all of this data for Norwich. The problem was between the lines: all of these inquiries were asking about "delinquent Norwich county taxes." Vermont is one of four states in the country that doesn't use the county system; all of its records are kept on a town/city basis. So it was apparent to Ms. Porter that something was awry, especially when she learned that all these inquiries were based on information contained on TRW credit reports.

Clue #2: Trans Union is the prevailing credit bureau in the Vermont region. Private Detective Porter is born and immediately opens an investigation. Okay, fine. Only three residents were denied credit before the problem was solved, but thanks to the alert work of Ms. Porter, everyone in Norwich was rescued from a potentially devastating situation.

What if she had not caught the error? What if it had gone undetected for weeks or even months? What impact could this have had on the lives of innocent residents damaged by clerical error?

Now what if this had happened to the entire city of Dallas? San Francisco? Chicago? New York?

What if this error weren't caught and an employer doing a routine employee background update found this incorrect tax lien information? Don't think it doesn't happen: defense contractors will check the credit records of employees with security clearances from time to time to make sure there are no potential breaches of security stemming from an employee who could be compromised due to financial problems. All of a sudden, an innocent employee is either demoted or relieved of duties—a victim of errors in the credit reporting system. A computer bullet in the back.

How do we know other instances of these types of mistakes aren't happening today?

The answer is simple.

We don't.

Stephen Gardner, former assistant Attorney General for the State of Texas, knows first hand about the accuracy of credit files. He's the person who initiated the lawsuit seeking class-wide recovery against TRW in 1991 alleging that the citizens of Texas were being harmed by the masses of incorrect information held in the TRW files. The suit was later joined by several other states and settled with TRW agreeing to begin a concerted effort to clean up their act, which included allowing Americans to obtain a copy of their credit report at a maximum cost of $7.50 (but in a smart public relations move, TRW is giving everyone one free copy of their report per year).

The Texas attorney general's office was able to get a look at the inner sanctum of TRW and learn that over 40% of the files contained some level of erroneous information. Other studies have put the estimate higher...closer to 50%. Your chances of having incorrect information in your TRW credit file were 1 in 2 as late as 1991!

In fairness to TRW, this incorrect information could be something as minor and mundane as listing a person as a "Junior" or "Senior" or living on "Pennant Drive" instead of "Pennant Boulevard."

Maybe being listed as a "Junior" when you're really a "Senior" isn't as minor as it first appears, either. As Mr. Gardner pointed out *"...the sins of the fathers may fall on the heads of the sons."* How many "juniors" have been plagued by their father's credit mistakes or, more accurately, how many fathers have encountered credit report problems because of their flaky sons?

However, the information could also be quite serious, such as incorrectly listing an account as charged off or a consumer having foreclosures or even tax liens.

TRW figured it out and their solution was simple. To right their wrongs, they purged tax lien information for files of consumers living in Vermont, New Hampshire, Rhode Island and Maine. Fair enough, right?

Wrong.

This opens another potential can of worms. What about those consumers that actually *have* and *deserve* tax liens?

This information is now erased and the file is now *incorrect by reason of omission.* So what happens if a bank lends money to a person in one of these states, and the person really does have some negative information like a tax lien that should be showing up and ends up defaulting on the loan? The bank loses because they made a lending decision based on incorrect information from the credit bureau.

Damned if you do and damned if you don't.

The mess in Norwich has a milestone ending: Jeffrey Amestoy, Vermont's Attorney General filed suit against TRW alleging violations of the state's Consumer Fraud Act, asking for $10,000 per violation. TRW settled the action (without admitting any wrongdoing), and paid the state of Vermont $125,000; 1,200 Vermont citizens were eligible to receive up to $1,000 each. The potential total bill for NDR's mistake: $1.2 million.

By the way, TRW has a new subcontractor working Vermont...Service Abstract. This company lists Dun & Bradstreet and Merchants Credit as clients, and its title examiners are trained by attorneys.

Take another case, the story of poor Michael G. Riley, a writer for *Time* magazine.

Mistakes in his records included an error courtesy of his friends at his local social security office. It seems that they were under the impression that he was deceased and issued a *"dead alert"* against his social security number. Being dead is as bad for a credit report as going through a bankruptcy.

Nobody wants to deal with a dead man.

Citibank didn't. They canceled his card. He didn't want to leave home without it (oh, wrong company).

Anyway after a month of playing tag with the good people at the Department of Health and Human Services, Mr. Riley signed an affidavit proclaiming that "...I am, indeed, alive and well....".

3

PUTTING THE BALL
INTO PLAY

"Trust everybody...but cut the cards."
–Finley Peter Dunne

YOU MUST START THIS GAME WITH ALL OF THE CARDS IN THE deck. This means you'll be contacting all three of the national credit bureaus that have been profiled in the previous chapters.

I realize that there may be local or regional credit reporting bureaus/agencies in your area, but these companies generally rely on the information collected by one of the "Big Three."

As a result of a settlement of a class action lawsuit initiated by the Texas State Attorney General's Office a couple of years ago, TRW agreed to give Americans one *free*[1] copy of their credit bureau report annually...just for asking!

---

1. If you have been turned down for credit within the last sixty (60) days, under the Fair Credit Reporting Act (which we'll discuss in greater detail later in this book) you are entitled to a free copy of your report, even if you've already received your annual free one from TRW. *That's the law*, but it only applies if you have been turned down for credit recently, and if the potential credit grantor used TRW as their source of information on which to base their opinion. Any "turndown" letter you may have received from potential credit grantors will state the source of information upon which they based their denial towards the bottom of the letter. This source must provide you with a free report if you request this report within sixty (60) days of the turndown.

What a deal! So send away for your *free* TRW report imme-diately, before proceeding any further with any attempts to evaluate your current credit profile.

And while we're still on the subject of TRW, you must be sure to include with your letter requesting a free copy of your credit bureau report some form of "positive identifica-tion." Their position is to "ensure privacy" so give them what they need, but *only* what they need. Here's what I mean. TRW will ask for:

- "...a copy of a proof of address document containing your name and current address."

- "...a current billing statement from a major creditor, a utility bill such as cable TV, gas, electric, water or tele-phone; or a valid driver's license issued with your cur-rent address."

Okay. So they're trying to protect your privacy, huh? Then give them only what they need: a cover letter from you with all of the appropriate information and a document showing your name and current mail/home/billing address. *But noth-ing else!*

That means that if you send them a copy of the first page of your telephone bill, use a black marker and black out the *entire* telephone number or any other account number; if you send them a copy of a utility bill, black out *all* account numbers (including those that may be encoded in a long, multinumbered sequence across the very top or very bot-tom of the bill). Same thing goes for any credit card ac-count statements.

And be sure to black out any account balance information, including balance owed and payment currently due. It's none of their business. Give them *only* what they requested. Nothing more. In short, you need to show TRW that you have a valid account, but you do not need to reveal information about the account.

If you decide to send them a copy of your current driver's license, be sure to black out the line of information containing your driver's license number. You may also choose to black out height, weight, eye color, hair color and other restrictions/information on your license. Finally, you may wish to black out your picture while you're at it. Remember, they wanted proof of identification with your current home/mailing address on it, so give it to them. But nothing else. It's none of their business, so why give them all of this additional information that they could potentially use, resell or put into their own computer data banks? It's none of their business. Don't forget this!

TRW ADDRESS/TELEPHONE NUMBER

As this first edition of *Life After Debt* goes to press (August '93), here's the current address/phone number for TRW. This could change and if it does, ask your local directory assistance operator for the local/regional TRW office that you need to consult.

TRW Complimentary Credit Report
PO Box 2350
Chatsworth, CA 91313-2350
(800) 392-1122

Remember, TRW can change their mailing address at any time so be sure to call their toll free number listed above first to make sure this address we are providing is correct.

If you wish to write to lodge a complaint or start your journey up the chain of command, try this address or phone number (phone numbers are always subject to change):

TRW
ATTN: NCAC
P.O. Box 2104
Allen, TX 75002
(800) 862-7654

Please use the Credit Bureau Report Request Letter form located in Appendix A at the back of this book to get your report, and follow the letter format provided.

CSC/EQUIFAX ADDRESS/TELEPHONE NUMBER

Again, CSC/Equifax services various parts of the country and the correct address to request a copy of your current credit bureau report could be different from region to region. CSC/Equifax isn't as charitable as our good friends at TRW so this report will cost you. But it's money well spent; you've got to know what everyone is saying about you (and your spouse if you're married) before you attack your current situation.

Here are two toll free numbers for you to call CSC/Equifax:

(800) 759-5979 or (800) 685-1111

If you want to write to them, try this address:

**PO Box 740241
Atlanta, GA 30375**

Again, CSC/Equifax will ask you for the usual data, including a copy of your current driver's license, but be sure to black out data that is impertinent to this process (like height, weight, eye color, hair color and other restrictions information).

CSC/Equifax will charge you for this report: An average fee of $8 is the prevailing rate and varies from state to state so call the 800 number first and get all of the specifics before you sit down to write your letter. (Remember, *Life After Debt* makes it really easy for you to get this report; to make this part of the process a no-brainer, use a copy of the Credit Beureau Report Request Letter form in Appendix B at the back of this book.)

By the way, when you send the money to CSC/Equifax for your copy of your report, I strongly urge you to send them a money order, readily available at the post office or convenience stores across the country.

Why?

When you send them a personal check, you're allowing a few things to occur:

- They may sit on your report for an extra 10-14 days waiting for your "check to clear" their bank;

- You're giving them all information that is printed across the front of your check;

- You're giving them the name, location/branch and account number of your checking account.

Am I sounding paranoid? Perhaps. But don't ever lose sight of the type of the business TRW, Equifax and Trans Union are all in: the collection, sale and resale of information on you.

The front of your check tells a story. It's up to you whether you wish to tell them your story...or not.

TRANS UNION ADDRESS/TELEPHONE NUMBER

They're the easiest and quickest to deal with if you've been turned down for credit recently. No 800-number here, but a voicemailtype, touchtone prompting system that gets your report out to you quickly.

Again, if you have been denied credit within the last thirty (30) days, federal laws dictate that they provide you a "freebie" report upon request. Contact them at their main consumer assistance number:

(313) 689-3888

Their main office address if you wish to write is:

**PO Box 7000
North Olmstead, OH 44070**

Trans Union also has three regional offices if you wish to

contact these in your part of the country:

PO Box 360
Philadelphia, PA 19105
(215) 569-4582

South First St., Suite 201
Louisville, KY 40202
(502) 584-0121

PO Box 3110
Fullerton, CA 92634
(714) 738-3800

The computer will prompt you and ask the basic questions: first name, last name, address, city, state, zip code, social security number, date of birth and finally, whether you've moved in the last 2 years (or not). They promise to send your report out within 72 hours. However, if you wish to simply obtain a copy of your report for your own personal information you'll need to send them $8 for one ($16 for a married couple) with all of the appropriate information as outlined above, with one addition:

They also want to know the name of your current employer and their telephone number.

As far as I'm concerned, it's none of their business. It is not relevant to your request for your information from their files.

Refuse to give it to them! Follow my form letter outlined in Appendix B at the back of the book, send them the appropriate amount of money in money order form and see what happens.

SUMMARY

Your first steps toward regaining control of your life begins with obtaining copies of all three of the national credit bureau reports:

TRW
CSC/Equifax
Trans Union

Get those reports in your hands and move ahead to your next challenge, but keep these facts in mind:

- There are over 1,100 credit and mortgage reporting companies in the United States
- There are more than 450 million credit files on American consumers
- 1 in 3 people who view their credit reports end up disputing information
- 75% of the those disputes were corrected by the credit reporting agency

If you don't know what your files say about you, you are blind and foolish. The chances are 1 in 2 that your files contain erroneous information!

Go get 'em!

4

THE AMERICAN CREDIT INFORMATION NETWORK: AN OVERVIEW

"Get your facts first,
then you can distort them as much as you please."
—Mark Twain

THIS PROBABLY WON'T SURPRISE YOU, but the credit reporting system used in the United States is the most complicated in the world.

At some point in everyone's life, they are subjected to some form of credit check. The federal law that governs how credit information is collected, distributed, reported and (supposedly) corrected in case of errors is the *Fair Credit Reporting Act* (FCRA), originally enacted by Congress as *Public Law #91-508* on October 26, 1970, effective April 24, 1971 and amended under *Public Law #95-598* on November 6, 1978.

You don't need to buy this book to find out your rights under the FCRA.

If that's why you bought it, take this book back and get them to refund your money *immediately!*

You can get a **free** copy of the law from any Federal Trade Commission office located across the country (yes, to make it easy for you. I've even provided a list of all of the regional FTC offices in Appendix Z in the back of the book).

A negative credit report can affect your life in ways most people don't even realize.

Did you know that if you apply for a job that pays $20,000 or more per year, a prospective employer can obtain a copy of your credit report without your authorization?

Did you know that if you apply for life insurance with a face amount of $50,000 or more that the insurance underwriter may obtain a copy of your credit report without your authorization?

Did you know that if you currently work in an industry that deals in such areas as national defense, hightech, computers or banking, that your employer probably already obtained a copy of your credit report without your authorization and that if a negative credit rating develops, you can be demoted or dismissed?

Did you know that many property and casualty insurance companies will refuse to underwrite your home or other personal property based on information from your credit report obtained without your authorization?

Scary stuff, huh? Big brother is alive and well in the 1990's.

As recently as May '93 the Federal Trade Commission

settled charges leveled against the retailer Marshall Field & Company over their alleged nonhiring of job applicants because of poor credit reports.

Under terms of the FCRA, job applicants must be told that they were not hired because of a poor credit record. Marshall Field's apparently failed to inform applicants of this, along with the name of the credit bureau that provided the negative information. And in some cases, Marshall Field's rejected applicants for one position but offered alternative employment based on their credit file.

Marshall Field's reached the settlement with the FTC "with no admission of violation of any laws or regulations," but what good did this do for those individuals who needed the job and had no idea why they weren't hired?

Oh well.

It is amazing how little the American public knows or understands about a system that affects us in virtually every part of our lives.

TRW, Equifax and Trans Union all utilize data management and complex algorithms to assist credit grantors' attempts to predict losses. Remember, these are only predictions... educated guesses used by loan portfolio managers to try to lessen the impact of potential losses due to consumer defaults or bankruptcies.

Because this is a system with an inherent margin of error, your only defense is your knowledge of its inner workings.

As I have said so many times on radio and television shows over the last year, **"knowledge is power"**; *Life After Debt* gives you the knowledge necessary to take control.

5

STARTING THE
CREDIT GAME

*"Money is better than poverty,
if only for financial reasons."*
–Woody Allen

MOST PEOPLE DON'T START OBTAINING CREDIT UNTIL THEIR EARLY 20's, although there is a frightening trend that has developed over the last few years. Many of the large national charge card issuers (like VISA, MasterCard and Discover) are opening accounts for college students with no visible means of support and incomes under $10,000 per year.

Incredible as it seems, these major banks are issuing cards to young adults who do not have a regular income and certainly not much experience in handling their finances and debt. More and more students are graduating from college with not only student loans to repay but huge balances of unsecured credit card debt.

The banks justify this insanity by charging 18-21.9% interest rates and betting that Mom and Dad will bail out their kids when they get in over their heads.

If you know someone who potentially fits this profile, talk to them early (like their senior year of high school) and counsel them on financial/debt management before it's too late!

Historically, your ability to obtain credit is based on your previous record/ability to handle it.

This means that your credit demands/desires for today and tomorrow will depend upon your performance of the last 7+ years. If you were a "slow pay" (meaning late according to the terms that were extended to you, usually over 30 days late) this will negatively influence any potential credit grantor for years to come.

A number of laws apply to consumers regarding the use of credit and I've included a brief description of these in Chapter Seven "Federal Laws You Need to Know." Be sure to read them to gain a clear understanding of what applies to your specific situation.

THE CREDIT APPLICATION

When you apply for credit you fill out a detailed credit application. Your prospective creditor asks you such questions as:

- Your employer (and their phone number and address)

- Your position

- Length of employment

- Annual, monthly or weekly salary

- Name of supervisor

- Your social security number
- Your home address and phone number
- Name/address/phone number of nearest relative
- Name/address/phone number of nearest friend(s)
- Name of your bank and your account numbers
- Name and account numbers of any other credit accounts
- Other information they may deem pertinent

Some of the information requested on this initial application is compiled for the sole purpose of finding you should you default ("skip-tracing") and is usually turned over to the collection department or outside collection agency. In fact it is common for the original creditor to attach a copy of this credit application to the file given to the debt collectors. If you've hit some tough times and are not able to pay your creditors as agreed, you shouldn't be surprised if your friends and neighbors start getting phone calls from people trying to find you. Remember, you gave them these names, addresses and phone numbers when you applied for credit; they're just doing their job trying to get you to pay your bills.

A prospective creditor has the right to ask you questions on a credit application and you have a right to refuse to answer them. If you don't want them to have all of this personal information, you don't have to give it to them, including your social security number (which we'll go into greater detail about later in this book).

<u>The punch line here:</u> the prospective creditor doesn't have to extend you any credit if you don't follow their guidelines when requesting credit on the initial application.

Furthermore, if you give any false information on the credit application you are breaking federal law and could be criminally prosecuted.

DEBT COLLECTOR CONTACTS

If you are getting calls from creditors at home or at work and don't know how to handle this situation, get your hands on a copy of ***BACK OFF!*** **The Definitive Guide To Stopping Collection Agency Harassment.** This is a valuable book that will show you how to take the debt collector out of the collection equation quickly and keep them from placing negative information on your credit report.

Something everybody <u>must</u> understand:

You are ***not*** required to give any informaton to someone just because they ask for it. If you do not desire to allow the creditor (or many times the debt collector) to "update" your credit file, you may refuse to do so. It doesn't matter if it's the original creditor calling or writing, their debt collector or their attorney.

The ***only*** time you are required to release this type of information is if you are involved in any type of judicial proceeding (civil or criminal) and are ordered by the court to divulge this information. Refusal to do so could result in contempt charges being brought against you and potential jail time. Challenge any attempt to collect this personal information from you at all times, with one important warning: If you want to increase a credit line/credit limit or a creditor wishes to periodically "update" your credit file and you refuse to answer their questions or submit updated financial statements/information, the creditor can and many times will:

- Reduce your credit line

- Close your account

- Call your note (accelerate repayment terms)

Remember this if you are on "friendly" terms with your creditor, or you may shoot yourself in the foot.

However, I'm assuming you've already ruined your credit rating (or are well on your way) or are a victim of mistaken credit identity and that's why you're reading this book.

WHAT ABOUT FILING FOR BANKRUPTCY?

Why do people file for bankruptcy? Almost of all of the individuals polled over the last couple for years have decided to go the route of last resort for one reason: to stop creditor harassment. Recent reports on programs like ABC's *"Good Morning, America"* or CBS's *"60 Minutes"* focused on the enormous debts under which many Americans are buried resulting from medical care. Inadequate or no insurance can quickly force consumers into insolvency and into the arms of attorneys specializing in bankruptcy.

Millions of Americans are choosing bankruptcy, being lured into the web by advertising touting:

"STOP CREDITOR HARASSMENT INSTANTLY!" or
"START OVER FRESH WITHOUT ANY DEBTS" or
even "GET A CLEAN START!"

Wrong. Wrong. And wrong.

Bankruptcy is the absolute *worst* thing any consumer can do to themselves. It can stay on your credit report for up to 10 years but in reality, will follow you to your grave forever.

When was the last time you looked at a credit application for a car or a home? That question, usually at the bottom of the page, is your question of doom: "Have you ever filed for bankruptcy?" If you don't answer it truthfully, you've committed a felony.

Over 95% of people who file for bankruptcy do so to (in their eyes) eliminate "creditor harassment" when in reality, they're really suffering from debt collector harassment.

Americans don't ever have to deal with a debt collector. Public Law 95-109, also known as the *Fair Debt Collection Practices Act*, gives consumers the right not to deal with debt collectors if they choose not to.

That's right: **you** can *fire* your debt collector.

And when you fire the debt collector, you are regaining control of your life. You're eliminating the source of irritation that drives so many people into the bankruptcy courtroom. Pick up a copy of ***BACK OFF!*** **The Definitive Guide To Stopping Collection Agency Harassment.** (ISBN 1-880-925-04-4), available at bookstores and libraries across the country, if you need to learn how.

It's easy to do and will help you regain your self-esteem since you won't have to deal with these parasites anymore; ***BACK OFF!*** allows you to get back on your feet financially and repay your creditors on terms that will benefit everybody.

And the debt collectors will **no longer** profit from it.

Take control. Take these parasitic debt collectors **<u>out</u>**.

6

SOCIAL SECURITY NUMBERS

"The creditor hath a better memory than the debtor."
–James Howell

This chapter affects **everyone** in the country.

Originally created in order to track retirement and disability benefits to be disbursed by the newly formed Social Security Administration during the depression in the 1930's, the nine digit Social Security Number (SSN) allows individuals educated in the structure of the system to know instantly:

- the region of the country from which your number was issued

- a system to spot falsified numbers quickly

- a starting point to search for old records such as school records, voting records, real estate information, etc.

The SSN has turned into a federal identification number for all Americans. Like it or not, this nine digit number will follow you (with few exceptions) to your grave. This nine digit number is the very center of the credit reporting universe.

Many employers who are familiar with the SSN issuance system can spot a questionable job application immediately. By knowing how the numbers are issued, an employer interviewing an employee claiming to be a lifelong Texas resident with a SSN beginning with 433 sees an immediate red flag:

433 series SSNs are issued in <u>Arkansas</u>!

This could be a major problem for our prospective employee.

It's possible that the person was a dependent of a parent who was serving in the military or other extenuating circumstances, but it certainly throws up a flag for the person in the know about SSNs.

REQUIRED USES OF YOUR SSN

According to federal law, you are required to disclose your SSN under the following circumstances:

- To credit earning into your Social Security account;

- For the purpose of identifying you in the filing and payment of both state and federal income taxes;

- When applying for a driver's license in many states across the country your number is now required, then placed in a "sub-file" to help local, state and federal police agencies identify you;

- As an identifier to be reported to the IRS (on a Currency Transaction Record) for any cash transactions in excess of $10,000. This is commonly required at race tracks and casinos, in addition to currency exchange houses and banks.

If you have children, the IRS now requires that you include a SSN for each child you take as a deduction on your annual federal tax return. Your SSN is also used as your identifier if you serve in the military, and many colleges and universities use the SSN as the account number/identifier for students and their transcripts.

THE "REGION" NUMBERING SYSTEM

The SSN system of distributing numbers is very similar to the Zip Code numbering system.

The very first rule is easy to remember: there are no SSN issued with consecutive zeros; therefore if you spot a "000" series in the first grouping, a "00" series in the middle or a "0000" in the last series of numbers, this SSN is invalid.

The first three numbers denote the area of the country from which your number was issued. Since there is no "000" prefix at this time (it is not assigned) the first zone is 001-003 for those numbers issued in New Hampshire. The numbers increase as they head west, going up to 626 for those issued in California. Exceptions include:

- Numbers in the ranges of 574, 580 and 586 issued to Southeastern refugees from April 1975 through November 1979;

- Numbers ranging from 700-728 are reserved for rail-road employees;

- Numbers ranging from 729-999 were unassigned as the book went to press in August, 1993.

A table showing Social Security Numbers and their issuance zones is listed in Appendix DD.

The second group of numbers are called the "group numbers" and are usually keys for those in the know to spot false SSNs.

These two digits break down the SSNs into more manageable groups for identification. Even though these numbers can represent groups starting at "00" and ending with "99", many sets of numbers have not yet been assigned/used. Any SSN with one of these (as yet) unused groups is instantly invalid.

The last of group of numbers is your serial number. This group can start from "0000" and end at "9999." These last four digits merely place a number in a group. Any combination is valid, as long as it is not the aforementioned "0000."

CLOSING THOUGHTS ABOUT YOUR SSN

Your SSN is the heart and soul of the information databases across the nation. Theoretically, your number is yours and uniquely yours alone. However, there have been cases documented of numbers being assigned twice, of vindictive ex-spouses getting even through the SSN databases, and other scenarios that are a nightmare for the person trying to straighten out their SSN related problems.

- Assume if someone asks for your SSN that they may obtain a copy of your credit report (with or without your consent).

- Challenge *anyone* requesting your SSN if they are not authorized to have your number. This means that if it isn't a bank/S&L, a government related agency or a law enforcement authority, **refuse to give out your number!**

The consequences of not giving out your SSN could be a refusal for goods or services you are trying to obtain, but be tough.

- Many schools have been known to issue "special" identification numbers to students who refuse to give out their SSN.

- Car rental agencies may request your SSN. *Refuse!* They won't rent a car to you unless they have a credit card (normally) and since the credit card issuer is the one that is taking the credit risk, it is no business of the car rental company to have your SSN.

- Many medical professionals require your SSN prior to extending services. If you are paying cash up front for the services about to be rendered or they have pre-approved insurance coverage and you are prepaying the deductible or co-payment, refuse to give them your SSN. It is none of their business.

Pertinent Social Security Number facts are outlined in Appendix CC for further reference.

7

YOUR RIGHTS
UNDER FEDERAL LAW

*"Law: An ordinance of reason for the common good,
made by him who has care of the community."*
–St. Thomas Aquinas

UNLESS YOU'VE GOT SOME BASIS FOR UNDERSTANDING the laws that govern the credit reporting industry, you're walking into an ambush of confusion. Here's a quick compilation of the laws that are important for consumers to know:

The Fair Credit Reporting Act (FCRA) establishes procedures for correcting mistakes on your credit record and requires that your records only be made available for legitimate business needs by those companies that have a right to know. The FCRA also dictates that these records be kept confidential. A credit record may be kept for 7 years and include your payment history, judgments, liens and lawsuits or other adverse information. Bankruptcies may stay on your credit record for 10 years. *If a consumer has been denied credit, they may receive a copy of the credit report used to deny their request for free within 30 days of denial.* (Refer to Appendix W)

The Fair Debt Collection Practices Act (FDCPA) is designed to eliminate abusive, deceptive and unfair debt collection practices. The FDCPA applies to any "third party debt collector" or those who use a name other than their own when collecting consumer debts. It also applies to any attorney who collects two or more debts per year. (Refer to Appendix Y)

The Equal Credit Opportunity Act (ECOA) requires all credit applicants be considered on the basis of their actual qualifications for credit and not be denied credit because of certain personal characteristics such as age, sex, marital status, race, color, religion, national origin or because you may receive some type of supplemental financial benefit such as veterans benefits, welfare, social security. Furthermore, you cannot be denied credit because you exercised your rights under federal credit laws such as filing a billing error notice with a creditor. (Refer to Appendix EE)

The Fair Credit Billing Act (FCBA) spells out procedures requiring creditors to promptly correct billing mistakes; FCBA allows you to withhold credit card payments on defective goods; it also requires creditors to promptly credit your payments. The FCBA (refer to Appendix FF) defines a billing error as:

- Any charge for something you didn't purchase or;

- A purchase made by someone without authorization to use your account;

- A purchase that is not properly identified on your bill;

- A different amount on your bill than the actual purchase price;

- A date different than the actual purchase date;
- Something you did not accept on delivery;
- A purchase not delivered according to your agreement;
- Errors in arithmetic;
- Failure to show a payment or credit to your account;
- Failure to mail the bill to your current address if you told the creditor of your address change at least 20 days before the end of the billing period;
- A questionable item or an item for which you need additional information/clarification.

Unsolicited Credit Cards. It is illegal for card issuers to send you a credit card unless you ask for or agree to receive one. This law was initiated to prevent unrequested cards from being intercepted in the mail and used. However, a card issuer may send, without your request, a new card to replace an expiring one.

Should you receive a solicitation in the mail offering you a credit card and they request either:

- your Social Security Number
- your signature

and you know your credit is bad...

DON'T DO IT!

It will only add insult to injury and show up as an additional "inquiry line" (which we'll discuss later) on your credit report, in addition to your being disappointed when they turn you down.

By the way...

Pre-approved credit card applications have become a way of life over the last decade and a new breed of criminal has found a new way to take advantage of this aggressive marketing technique. They're called "dumpster divers" and their goal is to find discarded solicitations in the trash, change your "address of record," sign your name and wait for their new card...in your name. Think about the mess this will create, and the potential for fraud and loss.

Do everyone a favor before you throw out your trash: tear up/shred any of these types of applications and avoid the nightmare.

8

SCORING YOUR CREDIT PROFILE

*"Character is made by what you stand for;
Reputation, by what you fall for."*
–Robert Quillen

CREDIT GRANTORS HAVE DEVISED A SYSTEM to score potential debtors before extending them credit.

Built around statistical data that is constantly changing, scoring changes as a result of the dynamics of the regional economies across the nation.

Back in 1986-88, consumers in Texas, Oklahoma, Louisiana, Arkansas, New Mexico and Colorado were "red lined" by the nation's lenders. The downturn in the oil and gas, real estate and banking/savings and loan industries caused lenders to look at any applicant from these states with a great deal of skepticism. Regions such as California and the eastern seaboard are now feeling some of the same wrath of bankers and bank regulators based on the performance of their region and not on their individual merits.

No matter when and where you are in the cycle, a de-facto scoring system exists as a tool to help credit grantors make their decisions.

Trans Union has a service they call EMPIRICA. In their own words:

> *(sic) "...EMPIRICA, the full-service point scoring system that doesn't stop at the line. Developed by Trans Union and Fair, Isaac, the world leader in point scoring model development, EMPIRICA delivers more than 'just a score' It includes monthly score distribution reports and an annual retrospective validation. With these unique benefits, EMPIRICA delineates delinquencies, slow-pays, no-pays and bankruptcies with greater accuracy for safer, more profitable credit decisions. Contact Marketing Services Dept., Trans Union..."*

Personal stability indicators that credit grantors evaluate include:

- Married or divorced?
- Children? Number of dependents?
- Your age group?
- Years at present residence?
- Do you own or rent?
- Years at present job?
- If married, is your spouse employed?
- Debt to income ratio?
- Type of profession?
- Skilled or unskilled?

- Professional or "blue collar"?
- Do you have a checking account?
- A savings account?
- An IRA or other investment account?
- Do you own a car? What year?
- Buying or leasing?

How you answer the subjects listed above will add points to your total score. Negatives that will knock your net score down include:

- Frequent address changes
- Frequent employment changes
- PO Box (mail drop or resident hotel) for mailing address
- Low income
- Employment regarded as unskilled labor
- Working at a newly established business
- Business address listed is same as home address
- Too many charge accounts
- Too few charge accounts
- Slow pay
- Charge off
- Debt collection activity

- High debt to income ratios
- Credit counseling history
- Bankruptcy (Chapter 7 or 13)
- Being deceased

I'm serious. "Death alerts" originated by the Health and Human Services Administration can sometimes be incorrect (refer to Michael G. Riley, Chapter Two).

When this government agency—responsible for social security numbers and corresponding benefits—confirms that a person has died, they notify the credit reporting bureaus that this number is now (literally) dead. What happens if there is a clerical error? A missed key-stroke? A transposition of numbers?

Oops!

Since every credit grantor has its own formulas for determining "credit worthiness," it is impossible to outline a standard scoring system. Rest assured that no matter how much "good" credit information appears on your credit bureau report, the positive likely will be negated by one or more "negative" lines of information listed above.

Everybody across the nation fits into at least one category, so don't think your situation is unique. It's practically impossible to go through life without one of these negative items happening to you at least once. When your world turned upside down for whatever reason (loss of job, divorce, accident or illness, etc.) you were forced to "re-prioritize" your bills and repayment responsibilities.

I do not intend to pass moral or ethical judgment, but let's recognize the simple fact that keeping a roof over your head, food on the table, electricity on and water running, are now a higher priority than paying your unsecured creditors.

That's life. That's the risk they took when they extended credit to you. In no way, shape or form do I suggest that you do not repay your obligations that you rightfully owe. However, you had <u>better</u> understand that **how** you repay them and the terms under which you repay them could affect you for at least the next decade.

9

COMMON TERMS USED ON CREDIT REPORTS

*"Without knowing the force of words,
it is impossible to know men."*
—Confucius

So WHY BURY YOU WITH A BUNCH OF TECHNICAL JARGON? All you really want is to see positive results on your credit report. Some basic information on all three credit reports:

- Name of credit grantor

- Credit grantor's address (TRW only for now)

- Your account number with credit grantor

- Description of history (TRW only for now)

- Date account opened

- Joint or individual account

- Payment type (installment or revolving)

- Credit limit

- Balance currently owing

- Balance past due

- Payment history

- Date file last updated by creditor

The version of your credit report given to prospective credit grantors is different than the "consumer version" now mailed to consumers requesting a copy of their TRW report.

This version will also show (like the old style TRW reports used to) whether the information reported to TRW is reported either manually (notated by an "M" in the far left margin) or autodata (notated by an "A" in the far left margin).

MANUAL vs. AUTODATA REPORTING

Major credit grantors such as bank card issuers Citibank, Chase Manhattan, etc. or American Express, and others such as GMAC, Ford Motor Credit, etc. will normally report consumer payment histories on autodata.

Autodata is an automatic computer tape monitoring system that is updated periodically, usually on a quarterly basis.

Manually updated information examples include tax liens, judgements, bankruptcies, etc. and are usually given to the credit bureaus by companies that routinely scan public records for these entries.

DISPUTATION OF
MANUALLY GATHERED INFORMATION

When a consumer asks a credit bureau to verify or confirm a negative entry, it forces the credit bureau to go back and manually reconfirm this information. Because of the volume of inquiries to the credit bureaus, it is almost impossible for them to have someone go to the courthouse and manually check to make sure this information is true and correct. The information got into the credit files as a result of independent contractors who specialize in the collection of public records information. But to reverify a disputed line of public record data, the credit bureau must either spend the money to have someone verify it or do it themselves. The volume of inquiries or disputes sometimes makes this a costly, if not impossible task. As a result under the Fair Credit Reporting Act, if it is not verified within 30 days (the 30-day rule) it must be removed.

Information given to the credit bureaus on tape (autodata) is much easier to verify. In fact, if a consumer is successful in getting the negative information removed due to the 30-day rule, many times it will reappear when the regularly scheduled autodata tape update is made.

OTHER KEY CODES

TRW has made tremendous progress making their reports more "consumer friendly," introducing a new format for consumer report copies in January '93.

Equifax and Trans Union so far are staying with their traditional reports that look like something encrypted by the CIA. You and I have to spend most of our time matching codes in hope of understanding what is being reported.

One of the common codes used by all three bureaus was the I/R codes, found on the right hand columns of the reports.

These supposedly tell about your payment history: The "I" represents installment loans (such as mortgages, automobile loans/leases, etc.) and the "R" represents revolving credit lines (such as those granted by major department stores or credit cards like VISA and MasterCard).

An installment loan is a pre-set, regular (and normally equal) payment, amortizing a loan over a period of time.

A revolving credit line has a spending ceiling and the payment varies, according to your remaining balance.

Revolving credit lines are normally the most difficult for consumers to paydown or payoff because they usually carry high interest rates and many consumers lack the discipline to pay them off and keep them paid off. They're very seductive spending instruments for consumers, and creditors have known for decades that these represent a long term stream of cash for their businesses.

When you see a notation that your car payment has been rated an "I2," this means that you have been 30 days late in the last rating period. The most these credit reports normally report is the last 24 months of your payment history. A "R9" means that your revolving line of credit, for example on your VISA card, is 8 months or more delinquent.

An "R9" or "I9" is the worst notation on any credit report. An account with these notations has almost always been referred to a collection agency and charged off as a bad debt.

10

REMOVING NEGATIVE REMARKS FROM YOUR CREDIT BUREAU REPORTS

"When gossip grows old, it becomes myth."
–Stanislaw Lec

BEFORE CONTINUING THROUGH THIS CHAPTER OF THE BOOK, please understand that this chapter is designed for the following consumers:

TYPE A: Those individuals with clean credit histories who are being destroyed by erroneous information. Examples of this include:

1. A father whose son is a "Junior" who has gotten into credit problems; these problems are now showing up on dad's credit report. Bad credit, judgments and bankruptcies are all being shown incorrectly on dad's credit report;

2. A son whose father has gotten into credit problems and these problems are now showing up on son's credit report. Bad credit, judgments and bankruptcies are all being shown incorrectly on son's credit report.

TYPE B: An individual who has a common first and last name and is being plagued by erroneous information from someone completely unrelated.

TYPE C: Someone who is the victim of "identity fraud", a situation wherein an unknown individual has acquired credit or lawsuits using an assumed identity based on the use of a stranger's social security number.

TYPE D: Those individuals with damaged credit histories who wish to pay off their debts but not be penalized by the inequities of the credit reporting system.

For TRW/Equifax accounts: In their continuing effort to become more "consumer friendly," TRW and Equifax now enclose a *CREDIT REPORT DISPUTE FORM* with copies of your credit report.

If you have numerous accounts that you are disputing, I suggest that you use their form to dispute one or two accounts on the first pass.

Go after the oldest accounts first (the same goes for the other two reporting agencies as well) and be humble. Be thankful for the opportunity to correct this information, and most importantly, be smart. In the credit industry, the key phrase is:

"OLD AND COLD."

This means that the older an account is, the colder the account is. The older and colder accounts are the ones that will be most difficult to verify. Thus the 30-day rule applies, and they come off your report!

You'll be feeling pretty cocky when you get your first report back with notations from the credit bureau now reading:

"ITEM DELETED. SUBSCRIBER DID NOT REPLY."

"ITEM DELETED. SUBSCRIBER DID NOT VERIFY."

Success! The negative information has been removed because the subscriber (creditor) did not respond within the required 30 day period.

Let the report lie there for 1-2 months before you make the next pass. On the next attempt, try using a handwritten cover letter (using one of the sample letter formats provided in Appendix H) and go after the oldest accounts on the report.

Cycle through the process until you reach the possible stalemate: a subscriber that verifies that you really are late! Or worst yet, they verify that they charged your account off!

If you reach this point on your report, move on to the next step in the rebuilding process: negotiating revisions with the original creditor. Read on...

NEGOTIATING REVISED CREDIT BUREAU INFORMATION FOR OPEN ACCOUNTS

These notations can be updated if you choose to be tough and negotiate with the creditor reporting them. Many times you'll have better luck negotiating a debt that has been charged off than you will one that is 60-90-120 days past due.

Many times the creditor will re-report your account if you make a substantial payment on the balance. The key here is:

NEVER TAKE <u>NO</u> FOR AN ANSWER.
BE PERSISTENT.

And when you are successful in getting the creditor to re-report your account information in exchange for a substantial payment or payoff of the account,

GET THIS AGREEMENT IN WRITING BEFORE YOU PAY THEM A DIME.

Use my letter example in Appendix G as your model for your settlement letter.

NEGOTIATING PAYMENT FOR OLD DEBTS

The key here is to try to negotiate with the original creditor, especially in the case of an account being charged off as a bad debt. Negotiate a settlement with the creditor through the mail and get them to sign a letter similar to the one in Appendix G, making sure they agree to remove all negative information from all credit reporting agencies in the U.S. They will do it. Don't let them convince you that federal law prohibits them from doing this because it's not true. They can delete any information they wish, and if you are persistent and firm, you can get them to agree to delete all derogatory comments from your reports.

Remember:

NEGOTIATE! Start low and work your way up...a nickel

on the dollar is a good starting point. Don't forget: this is a bonus in their eyes since they've already written your account off, and they're willing to accept in many cases less than 100 cents on the dollar.

I am not going to pass moral or ethical judgments here, but simply inform you of the rules of the game and enlighten you about your options when repaying these old debts. If you feel better about paying 100 cents on the dollar and can afford it, by all means I encourage you to do so.

Again, never negotiate with a debt collector. Only deal with the original creditor, since they are the only one authorized to remove negative information.

If you don't get them to agree to the terms (outlined in the sample letter in Appendix G) in writing first, they will get a case of amnesia and you're screwed. Get them to put it in writing that they will remove this information from your credit report when you pay them the agreed amount before paying them a dime; otherwise, you've given away any negotiating leverage you had.

Why does this technique work?

Don't think you can pull this off because you are so persuasive. Whoever runs the credit/credit reporting department in question has heard just about every story under the sun. What will get you results is the same thread that runs through the credit and collections industries:

GREED.

The credit manager is in the business of collecting accounts receivable from their customers/clients. If your account was charged off a long time ago, the company has already taken the hit; they've already written off your account as uncollectible and deducted it as a loss under the "Bad Debt" category.

This means that whatever they collect is a bonus. The credit manager is a hero and you feel better about yourself. What does it cost for the credit manager to delete any negative information from your credit report?

Zero. Nada. Nothing. *Zilch*.

The credit/collections manager **will** play ball...eventually. And if they don't, this entry will fall off of your credit report after 7 years anyway. That's the law.

It doesn't cost anything to try. You'll be surprised with the results. Trust me. It works. I've done it.

DISPUTING PHANTOM COMPANIES

One of the pieces of fallout from the 1980's is the number of companies that either went under or were acquired in distress sales.

Many credit card companies, banks and savings and loans fit into this category. Once the bankruptcy courts, the old FSLIC, FADA or the RTC gets involved, you can bet that everything is going to get very complicated.

Many times when consumers make a pass to settle old credit card debts but find that their original issuing company has sold its portfolio of credit card accounts, their attempts to make good on an old debt go for naught.

Since the account has already been written off and the portfolio disbursed, it is sometimes impossible for a consumer to find anyone to take their money.

In these cases I suggest the consumer circle the negative information on their credit report with a wide tipped, red felt pen and write beneath this line of negative information *one* of the following in bold letters:

"THIS IS NOT CORRECT. PLEASE VERIFY."

"PLEASE INVESTIGATE! INCORRECT!"

"THIS INFORMATION IS INCORRECT. REMOVE!"

The consumer must attack these items for one simple reason: If no one is willing to take the consumer's money to settle the outstanding account, I promise you there is no one available to authorize the removal of the negative information (refer to the sample letter Appendix H). Now the consumer is expected to suffer the statutory 7 years until it falls off (according to the Fair Credit Reporting Act) because the original creditor is not available to negotiate with?

I don't think so.

That is the essence of getting old/outdated information off of your credit report. Challenge it off. Dispute it. The system cannot handle the surge of mail disputing information on a credit report under its current structure.

With all of the mergers/acquisitions in the last 10 years, the companies cannot verify the information in many cases.

So it comes off.

HANDWRITTEN CORRESPONDENCE... THE PERSONAL TOUCH

Unfortunately, if you decide to begin taking steps to clear negative information from your credit report and your letter looks too slick, it can raise suspicions.

Mix up your styles when writing to the credit reporting agencies. Same goes for letters to original creditors. If they perceive your letter as being too professional and too pretty, they may suspect one or more of the following:

- Credit clinic intervention
- Law office intervention
- Secretarial service intervention
- Personal secretary handling your letters
- You've got money/resources
- All of the above

If you're typing the letter, use a manual typewriter. Word processors and laser printers smell like money to me, and they'll smell like money to the credit bureaus or creditors, too.

Handwritten notes are also effective. That personal touch is disarming and appears sincere.

And if you're sending routine disputation letters to the credit bureaus, DO **NOT** SEND THEM VIA CERTIFIED MAIL! This is a red flag! The key to getting results is maintaining a level of innocence in your correspondence and expressing a desire to get these apparent mistakes cleared up as soon as humanly possible. Understand?

CERTIFIED MAIL

There will be times when a certified letter is necessary, such as genuine instances of erroneous information in your file. When you are absolutely right and you know that the information in your file **DOES NOT** belong to you, be very assertive, very professional and very tough with the credit reporting bureau. In case you forgot, there are estimates that over 50% of the files contain erroneous information. (Refer to Appendix D)

Give them 30 days from their receipt of your letter (yes, this is one of those times you need to send your letter via certified mail) to get the garbage off of your report. Failure to do so will result in your filing a lawsuit against the credit bureau, in addition to filing complaints with the proper state and federal agencies that enforce laws pertaining to fair credit reporting.

Refer to the sample demand letter to the credit bureau in Appendix T. In this case, I urge you to make this letter look as professional as possible. Laser printed correspondence will have the most impact; however, a clean, properly typed letter will work. And be sure to send it via certified mail.

INFORMATION OVERLOAD

I could hammer you with a million and one tips about massive disputation techniques, but let's get to the heart of the matter.

For whatever reason, your credit bureau report is screwed up. This book shows you how the system works and the steps you can take immediately to regain control of your personal financial situation. When conventional methods of dealing with the credit bureaus aren't getting you the results you desire, then it's up to you to play the game to win.

MORE ISN'T BETTER

Don't get carried away with the information you just learned. If you start sending out truckloads of dispute letters with the hope of cleaning up your credit report, the credit reporting bureaus have the right to reject any claims you have under the *"frivolous and irrelevant"* (FCRA §611(c)) portion of the law.

In other words, if they detect you have hired a credit repair clinic (which are usually scams out to take your money and unable to guarantee results) or they think you are trying to bombard and overwhelm the credit bureaus with paperwork so that they'll never make the 30-day rule, they'll trash your requests.

Another word about credit repair clinics, otherwise referred to as a "third party." The credit bureaus can legally ignore your requests if they detect that you're using one. Remember, under the law a creditor (or a debt collector) is not allowed to discuss your account with any unrelated third party without written authorization. If a credit clinic shows proof of authorization from you, the credit bureaus will almost certainly throw it out under the "frivolous and irrelevant" clause.

Don't try to rush the healing process! You didn't screw your credit report up overnight... you're not going to fix it overnight either. Relax. Haste makes waste.

The K.I.S.S. philosophy works here: _Keep It Simple, Stupid._ The tools I have given you will work if you are _patient_ and trust the strategies outlined.

11

INQUIRIES

Guess what can kill a credit report as quickly as bad credit?

Excessive inquiries.

An inquiry is a line of information, usually at the end of your report that shows who has received a copy of your credit report.

Every person/company (in theory) with access to the credit bureau database system has an identifier. Unique only to that person or company (like your social security number is to you) this company-subscriber name/number will show up on your report for 2 years from the date of inquiry.

It's a tool of the trade the lets potential lenders know if you're shopping for multiple credit lines. If you're out applying for a bunch of charge cards, you're sending a warning signal to anyone evaluating you as a potential credit risk.

<u>A rule of thumb:</u> no more than 6 inquiries per year. Any-

more sends up a red flag—the kind that encourages a potential lender to decline your request for credit.

Furthermore, if a credit analyst sees that you've applied for cards from Sears, American Express, JC Penny and Citibank VISA 12 months ago but your report doesn't show any accounts with any of these creditors, their next logical question has to be: *Why?*

Why did Sears and American Express turn you down? What do they know that I don't? Hmmmm. Better be safe.

Declined.

SHOPPING FOR A CAR?

John and Jane Doe are shopping for a new car. They hit 8 or 9 dealerships the first day, shrewdly negotiating to buy their next dream car. In order to get the salesman's attention, they need to appear serious.

The salesman asks some innocent questions and comes back in a few minutes ready to get down to business. What John and Jane don't realize is that they've probably just been hit with an inquiry on their credit bureau report. Contrary to popular belief, some people will obtain a copy of your credit bureau report **without your written consent!**

Guess what John and Jane did to themselves? They just got hit with 8-10 inquiries that will stay on their credit reports for 2 years from the date of the inquiry. They're screwed.

The moral of the story: Don't give out any information about yourself to anyone. Use only first names. Never give out your social security number, because they will use it to qualify you.

REMOVAL OF EXCESSIVE INQUIRIES

Unless you have given someone written permission to obtain a copy of your credit report, you have the right to dispute this off of your report. Use the letter model in Appendix M to put this ball into play. And stand your ground. Use the follow-up letter (as shown in Appendix N) to get these unauthorized inquiries off of your report.

Individuals familiar with this part of the law feel that a verbal authorization is sufficient. The test for furnishing a report in these circumstances is that your report can be released to anyone the reporting agency has reason to believe "intends to use the information in connection with a credit transaction involving the consumer..." (FCRA §604(3)(A)).

I contend that if you have not given someone your verbal authorization and the other party cannot prove that there was a possible credit transaction, the credit bureau must remove this information. Now that you're almost finished with this chapter, you know better than to give anyone sufficient information to pull a copy of your report. Right?

Some caveats to this rule...
The following folks do not need your written consent to obtain a copy of your report:

- An existing creditor
- The IRS
- A party that has a judgment against you

Everyone else had better provide you or the credit bureau with a signed release from you authorizing them to obtain a copy of your report. If not, the credit bureau *must* remove the inquiry.

12

YESTERDAY'S SPOUSE; TODAY'S CREDIT NIGHTMARE

"I never hated a man enough to give his diamonds back."
−Zsa Zsa Gabor

STUFF HAPPENS.

People grow apart.

Goals change.

Adversity raises its ugly head and tests (and sometimes breaks) the bonds of a marriage, and the only people who profit are the divorce lawyers.

When two people form that ultimate partnership they usually do so with no thought of having to split the assets at some time in the future.

Nor do they consider how they may have to divide the liabilities, either.

"I GOT MY NEW SOCIAL SECURITY CARD TODAY..."

The first steps normally taken in the fledgling marriage are those to the local Health and Human Services office for the new wife to officially change her name. You know the

73

game...joint checking and savings accounts... joint credit cards...joint ownership in the cars and new home. It's a partnership, right?

One out of two isn't bad. With divorce rates stabilizing around 50% over the last decade, it all boils down to this sobering thought:

You have a 1 in 2 chance of using a divorce lawyer to split your assets, all liabilities and all of your responsibilities if you have any children.

Who wants to plan for failure?

Nobody, which makes it even more difficult to untangle the web of debts when splitting a relationship.

Community property laws vary from state to state, as do laws governing alimony/spousal support, etc. As always, consult with a qualified divorce attorney and please, check their credentials first before signing them on.

There are divorce attorneys who specialize in keeping both parties upset and off balance in the interest of churning their fees and keeping that stream of cash from you flowing, so be careful.

GET A POST OFFICE/MAIL DROP BOX

First things first. You need a safe place to receive correspondence from creditors, bank statements, etc., so spend the money and get a post office or mail drop box. The last thing you need is a disgruntled or emotionally wounded spouse intercepting your mail and new credit cards. Be safe now so you won't be sorry later.

JOINT DEBT OBLIGATIONS

If you are heading for divorce, be sure to get your house in order early. By this I mean that it is important to make sure that any assets that you are entitled to but your spouse is not should be segmented into accounts that your spouse has no access to.

Consider opening a new checking/savings account in your name that only you have access/signatory rights to. You may wish to open this new account in a different bank. After all, banks are managed by people. And people talk.

Even more crucial than moving cash or other negotiable securities/assets to a safe status only you control is the disposition of all joint credit cards. These can be just as dangerous as cash, since they represent debt obligations for either party. There have been rumors flying for years about the horrors of a disgruntled spouse armed with credit cards. Don't test your soon-to-be-ex-spouse's pain or revenge threshold. The results can be devastating.

WHEN YOU KNOW YOU'RE SPLITTING UP, TURN OFF THE CARDS!

Contact the credit card company on the phone and notify them that you are about to dissolve your marriage. Ask them to close the current account and open a new account in your name only. Believe me, the credit card companies are very familiar with these situations and would much rather keep you as a happy, satisfied and financially performing customer than have their debt collections department chase you or your ex-spouse for the balance on the old account. Don't invite disaster...turn the cards off (use the sample letter format in Appendix I).

If you have a card with a $5,000 limit and $2,000 balance, the credit card company may issue you a card with only a $1,500 limit. This reflects the original $5,000 limit less the current $2,000 balance, leaving a net available limit of $3,000. Split two ways that gives you your own new card with a $1,500 limit. However, it is not out of the question for a credit card issuer to cut your limit if it fears you may suffer from severe financial distress resulting from this change in your life. They may be doing you a favor.

You don't need to be running up any huge debts if you're moving through this phase of life, anyway. A lower limit may be a blessing in disguise and keep you from your own worst enemy...

You.

Especially on those days when you're depressed and buying some new clothes or electronic gadgets brightens your mood...until you get the bill. Be smart. Don't spend unnecessarily when you're going through this difficult period. But eliminate your potential liability with your soon-to-be-ex and turn off those joint cards.

Do it now !

REMARKS FROM YOUR PAST

It is not uncommon for the credit bureaus to "merge" spouses' credit files. Anytime two people use each other's income on a credit application to qualify for the loan, there is almost a 100% chance that the two files will merge on each of their individual credit reports. There are thousands of cases documenting two people who have been divorced by the courts for years, but are still married in the credit records.

If a couple refers to the other's income to buy a car and both individuals sign the note or lease agreement, both parties are on the hook, regardless of what any divorce court decree with a judge's signature says. All the divorce documents do is outline the terms of agreement between the couple; the divorce documents do not get either party off the hook for any joint debts or liabilities. (Refer to Appen-   dix J.)

<u>For example:</u> Ward and June Cleaver have been married for 25 years and finally decide that they're not compatible. They've raised two boys who have moved on with their lives...you know the scenario. They end up in divorce court.

The judge awards Ward the house; June gets the car and a couple years later Ward goes through midlife crisis. Ward lets the house go into foreclosure and forces the mortgage company (Mayfield Mortgage Company) to repossess the BEAUTIFUL house and sell it off. If there is any deficiency (i.e. excess monies owed) the mortgage company will go after not only Ward (who got the house in the divorce) but June, too! She was on the line for the house so they will come after her.

It might not be fair, but life isn't fair sometimes, is it?

WHY NOT JUST REFINANCE?

Sounds like a great idea, especially when interest rates are low, but it's not always an option if:

- Your financial situation has deteriorated.

- Property values have declined (anybody out there own a condo?).

- You have negative information on your credit report.

If you can refinance the ex-spouse off of the note, do it. Otherwise, some aggressive and creative negotiation may be in your future.

Learn from June Cleaver's mistake: Negotiate with the mortgage company/note holder to remove you from any liability on the note. Explain the situation and ask that they remove you as a service; sometimes they'll do it for free...but don't expect it. Do expect them to ask for a current financial statement. (Refer to Appendix K)

It's possible that they will release you from the note, but if they won't, just remember: Everybody's got a price, and most mortgage holders will play ball if you make a payment to principal. For example, the Cleavers owe Mayfield Mortgage a balance of $50,000. June's attorney is smart enough to make a pass at getting her released from the note and offers $500 additional payment to principal.

That $500 represents 1% of the total monies owed/outstanding on the mortgage and many times, this will be acceptable, really more as a token of good faith release than anything else.

Be prepared to increase the stakes and willing to pay as much as 10% of the balance owed in order to secure a release. In the Cleaver's case, this would be $5,000 paid to principal for June's release.

Who pays?

Ward should. He's got the house...if he wants the divorce, he pays to get June released from any potential liability. Period. Don't agree to the divorce unless you're "off the line."

WHAT ABOUT CREDIT CARDS THAT AREN'T YOURS?

Many times an ex-spouse's credit card will show up on a credit report even if there was no actual written liability for that card.

Again, this frequently happens from the "merging accounts" syndrome that occurs when two people marry. Use the letter in Appendix L to clean this up. It works very well, but be prepared for the process to take at least 60 days. The major banks are pretty good about it (Citibank responded very promptly and courteously in a recent case) and are usually willing to work with consumers facing legitimate misinformation dilemmas.

13

COLLECTION AGENCY NEGATIVE INFORMATION LINES

"A single lie destroys a whole reputation of integrity."
–Baltasar Gracian

REMEMBER WHEN VITO FROM KNEE BREAKER COLLECTION Agency called you and threatened to screw up your credit for 7 years?

Unfortunately, he wasn't kidding. There it is, plain as day on your credit report. Is this fair?

No. Vito is merely a hired gun for ABC Department Store, out trying to make a quick buck scaring people into paying him. ABC Department Store already wrote off your account, so you've got one bad mark against you.

Now Vito comes in with his gun to your head telling you to pay him or else. Adding insult to injury, you now have two lines of negative information on your report for one transaction.

Did you set out to open an account with Knee Breaker Collection Agency? Of course not.

No way. You will only pay the original creditor because these are the people who can change the information on your credit bureau report. Changing the information includes being able to delete the information. If you pay Vito, he has no control over what the original creditor will/won't report.

The catch here is that the original creditor has the ability to not only remove their line of negative information but can force Vito to remove his line of information, too.

Vito will tell you this isn't correct. He'll tell you that you've got to deal with him. Wrong on both counts. Remember, Vito gets a commission on everything he collects, so he'll say whatever it takes to get to get you to pay him.

Take him out early. If you haven't seen it already, get yourself a copy of **_BACK OFF!_** and follow those directions on how to handle the debt collectors.

The secret to removing collection agency activity on your credit bureau report is to make its removal a condition of the new terms you're negotiating with the original creditor.

Refer to Appendix O and use this letter as your model to handle collection agency information lines.

14

THOSE OUTRAGEOUS MEDICAL BILLS

"God heals, and the doctor takes the fees."
–Benjamin Franklin

WHETHER YOU ARE ONE OF 30 MILLION AMERICANS without health insurance, or a victim of deductibles, co-payments or even insurance company errors, medical bills can be as vexing as any other debt dilemma facing consumers today.

Hospitals face tight budgets and need to keep an eye on their cash flows very closely. As a result, many hospitals are unwilling to work with a former patient for an extended period of time. In fact, it is not unusual for a hospital to factor a portfolio of accounts receivable.

Factoring means that they sell off those accounts that are owed to them at a discount. For instance, let's assume they have $100,000 worth of receivables owed to them for the month of April. They really need the cash, so they sell these accounts to XYZ Financial at a discount. The hospital gets $90,000 today instead of having to collect all of the accounts from insurance companies or individuals. XYZ Financial has the incentive to collect 100% of that $100,000 worth of accounts...that's where they make their profit!

As a result, medical bills can be very unforgiving. Whoever holds your account isn't interested in any stories; they just want their cash.

You have a responsibility to make good on your debt; however, you do not deserve to be penalized on your credit report for at least the next 7 years, right?

After all, did you plan to go get hit by that car?

I doubt you woke up one morning and said to yourself, "Gee. I'm going to go run up some enormous medical bills today. Let's see if I can get run over by a car."

Of course not. Sometimes, things just happen. The last thing you need is to add insult to injury with the added discomfort of debt collectors and lousy credit hanging over your head.

If this situation sounds like something you've encountered or something a friend or relative is enduring, read on.

RECOVERING FROM MEDICAL BILLS

Again, if you received services from a doctor or hospital, you owe them the money. Or do you?

Believe it or not, hospitals and doctor's offices can make mistakes. I mean it. They really can! So the first step after you get hit with a huge medical bill is to make sure it is correct.

Speaking from experience, it is possible for hospitals to double-bill you for things like recovery room charges, hospital room charges, monitoring equipment, etc. It happens.

Step 1: Look over your bill closely and make sure that there aren't any errors. If you suspect there are errors, point these out to your insurance company. Obviously if you are paying all your bills yourself, there is even more incentive here to make sure your bill is accurate. Use the letter model in Appendix V to request an audit of your account.

Step 2: If you are facing an enormous bill from the hospital, contact them first about working out repayment terms that you can handle. Be candid and explain your financial situation. And deal at the top of the ladder...don't try to deal with those people in accounting or collections; they do not have the authority to negotiate a deal. Go to the top. Start at the chairman or president's office, and send them a letter modeled after the one in Appendix P. Make sure you send the letter via certified mail.

Step 3: If they ignore you (always a possibility) and refer your account to an outside collection agency, get a copy of **_BACK OFF!_** and follow those instructions. It will work and the account will be referred back to either the original creditor or whoever owns your account (assuming they may have sold it off to a company like XYZ Financial discussed earlier in this chapter).

Step 4: Once you get back to whoever owns your account, negotiate using the same steps outlined earlier in this book.

Make sure that before you pay them a dime, you get them to agree in writing (using the letter modeled in Appendix G) to accept payment terms which include non-reporting of this account to any credit bureau in the U.S.

This same strategy will work with doctors, too. And speaking of doctors...

DOCTORS: THE BUSINESSPERSON...THE MYTH

Doctors are basically a good bunch of folks. Not necessarily the best businessmen as a whole, but some of us couldn't have made it this far without them.

However, there are some greedy ones out there who try to gouge the system wherever they can. Their fees are outrageous and they know they can always hammer you on your credit report if you don't pay up. Here are some facts to consider:

1. Doctors bill insurance companies for procedures on a fee schedule that is standard for their area. Their favorite term is "usual and customary" charges for whatever procedure they perform.

2. Some doctors don't pay much attention to these schedules. In fact, they look at the schedule as a starting point from which to build their fee structure. They'll bill your insurance company and take whatever payment they receive and badger you for the rest...if you

let them get away with it.

3. Many times insurance companies will sit on accounts as long as possible before paying them. It's the old "time is money" game to them...the longer they sit on their funds, the less expensive your claim becomes. In the mean time, your credit report could be going to hell in a hand basket.

4. If you suspect your doctor/health care provider is trying to stick it to you, contact the local AMA chapter covering your area. If there is not a local AMA-type association, there may be a similar organization designed to police the medical/health care provider community.

5. Ask them for a schedule of typical medical fees for the procedures you have been billed. Have your bills from your doctor/health care provider ready, since they may request certain billing codes in order to match up the information exactly. Many times the fees can vary within the same city depending on the doctor's *zip code*! I'm not kidding, certain zip codes are in the medical districts and can command higher fees.

That's why many times it is common for a doctor who specializes in anesthesiology to have a billing service with a more profitable zip code. Remember, anesthesiologists don't need an office...they don't have patients! They knock you out on the table and keep you alive with no overhead (except for their billing service and malpractice insurance). Now you know why these guys in particular wear masks.

6. Challenge their bills in writing! Use the letter modeled
in Appendix R and send it certified mail. Just because
they say you owe them doesn't mean you rightly owe
the debt! Try to work it out, try to reach a compromise.
And again, be sure to get all agreement in writing before parting with another dime! Once you pay them,
you lose any leverage you may have had and they get
a quick case of amnesia.

A former friend of mine used to say "Doctors have two
things that I can waste: *time* and *money.* They hate lawsuits,
so use the only leverage you've got if they aren't reasonable in clearing up a disputed debt."

**Some closing thoughts to the doctors/medical business
people of America:**

You've got a tough job dispensing medical advice while the
threat of potential malpractice litigation always lingers in
the back of your mind. But the bottom line here is that you
are in business to make a profit, and should be paid for your
services (as long as the charges are reasonable).

However, if you are not facing an emergency situation and
you accept the word of a total stranger that they will make
good on any invoice you present to them, you have made
the decision to treat them at your own financial risk.

If your business office staff doesn't think it's important to
pre-qualify patients to make sure they have adequate insur-

ance coverage and to clarify any deductible or co-payment before you see them, then perhaps you should consider a change in staff.

Ultimately, your office is accepting the credit risk if you fail to qualify your patients prior to rendering services. It takes two parties to complete a credit transaction.

The decision is yours.

15

STUDENT LOANS:
YOU PLAYED...YOU PAY!

"Credit is a system whereby a person who can't pay gets another person who can't pay to guarantee that he can pay"
- Charles Dickens

Argghhh!

Remember when you signed on the dotted line for that cheap money so you could go to college? You had a good time . . . you even fit 4 years of college into 6 years! Hey, it was cheap money, you learned enough to get your degree, and you made friends who will last a lifetime, right?

If you don't take repayment of your student loan seriously, paying for that opportunity to make those friends and have a 6-year party could last a lifetime.

Under the Bush administration, the federal government received authorization to begin offsetting federal income tax refunds for defaulted student loans. You know they're serious when the government can start garnishing your paycheck for non-payment in a state like Texas. Texas has the most protective laws on the books designed to insulate debtors from creditors. Yet even Texas residents can now feel the wrath of the Department of Education's efforts to recover more than $15 billion in defaulted student loans. Consider these facts from the Department of Education:

- Student loans are the third most profitable type of lending, beating out both car loans and mortgages.
- Most loans are "risk free" to the lenders, since the government guarantees repayment.
- Since the government guarantees repayment, few lenders put any effort into collecting them.
- If a borrower defaults the government makes good on the loan, plus interest, and the lender avoids the expense of servicing the loan. I ask you—where's the incentive for lenders to screen properly to make the loan, or to make any concerted efforts to collect it?

YOU PLAYED. YOU PAY.

If you played, you've got to pay. That's the bottom line here. However, there are some extenuating circumstances that need to be addressed:

a) With the "easy money" available to young adults from the various federal and state loan programs, a number of scams surfaced. Vocational schools promised young adults qualified training and easy job placement after course completion. In a number of cases, these schools were complete frauds that never delivered on promises, and students were left in debt with nothing to show for their efforts except a stream of debt collection notices and a credit nightmare that won't go away. Finally there's good news! If you can prove that you were deceived or defrauded by the institution, and misled about what they would deliver after you completed the course study, them Department of Education wants to hear from you! There's a way out, but you've got to contact them at once.

b) How many young adults right out of high school know anything about debt and credit? How many young adults balance their checkbook? (For that matter, how many older Americans balance their checkbook?) Yet we're allowing 18-year-olds to sign their life away without understanding the full ramifications of their signature on those documents.

So now it's time to repay the lender the money they are RIGHTFULLY OWED. Nine months out of school and no job? Too bad. Those monthly invoices start piling up. What do you do? You owe the money, but with your entry level position, you can barely make ends meet.

Good news! Thanks to Public Law 103-66, the Student Loan Reform Act, there are now a variety of ways that students can avoid the headaches associated with being unable to handle high student loan payments. From Alternative Repayment Plans to Income Contingent Repayment Plans that base the payment amount on the borrower's Adjusted Gross Income, now there's a light at the end of the tunnel— and it's not a train anymore.

c) Maybe you've already joined millions of other Americans and defaulted on your student loan. Did you read the fine print on those loan documents you signed 5 years ago? I didn't think so. Many student loan agreements include provisions for the lender to add an additional 43% to your balance owed if the account goes to a debt collector. Forty-three percent! This is starting to make the loan sharks sound good now. How can you ever pay this debt off? Contact the Department of Education and get ready for some good news.

SOME POSITIVE SOLUTIONS
CONGRESS HAS FINALLY ENACTED

Thanks to the Clinton Administration's efforts, the Student Loan Reform Act became operational on July 1, 1994. Some of the benefits of these reforms include:

1) Tighter regulations for student loans for non-traditional institutions of higher learning. There are some fine vocational institutions out there, but there are some outright scams floating around that spoil it for everyone. These are finally being controlled. The federal government is now making these non-traditional secondary education institutions adhere to reasonable but stringent guidelines for students to qualify for financial assistance.

2) In the reformed repayment program, there are now provisions that allow students enrolled in a school that becomes insolvent to be relieved from their obligation.

3) Thanks to direct lending programs created by these reforms, the cost of these loans will be reduced. Borrowers can now contact a central clearing house to discuss all aspects of their debt. The ability to restructure debts into a variety of repayment plans, with some payouts now extended as long as 30 years, should take even more pressure off not only yesterday's but tomorrow's students.

4) Defaulted student loans now in the hands of debt collectors can be renegotiated to new, attainable terms. Once the borrower has eliminated the third-party debt collector (as explained in *BACK OFF!*), they may take advantage of new provisions to allow the re-reporting of these loans after the timely repayment of their student loan over a 12-month period that allows borrowers to get back on their

feet, re-enter the student loan repayment system and not be penalized for years to come.

SOME ADDITIONAL IMPROVEMENTS
I'D LIKE TO SEE...

Our lawmakers did a world of good . . . but I'd still like to see some additional improvements to the student loan system that would include the following:

1) Require that every high school graduate to pass a basic consumer literacy test. I'm not trying to make Harvard MBAs out of high school graduates, but I believe today's graduates of either high school or college are woefully under-prepared for the simplest form of finance: balancing a checkbook. Keep it simple, but make sure students understand what a debt obligation is and how it will affect them over the long haul.

2) Require every borrower to watch a 15-minute video presentation explaining the document they are about to sign and their obligation to repay all monies borrowed. Make sure they understand that this is a debt they must honor, and don't allow borrowers to rush them through the fine print. (Student borrowers have got to understand what they're signing.)

3) President Clinton has proposed a government jobs program that will allow student loan borrowers/graduates to work off their obligation. Many states have similar programs in operation, allowing borrowers to work off their debt if they become teachers, for example. In short, certain job arenas excuse student debt. This is a good idea and a viable solution to the current crisis of defaulted loans.

4) Quit reimbursing lenders 100% for defaulted student loans. 75% reimbursement on defaulted loans is reasonable. I promise you they won't be making as many flaky loans as they have been in the past.

5) Allow the interest on student loans to be deductible, like home mortgage interest. Getting a post-secondary education in the 1990s is an expensive proposition, especially if an MBA, a law degree or (the granddaddy of them all,) a medical degree is the goal. Balances exceeding $100,000 aren't unusual anymore, so let's give tomorrow's leaders and professionals a fighting chance.

Since 1986 the U.S. Department of Education has forwarded over 10 million names and corresponding account information to the IRS to withhold tax refunds and pay off a portion of the student loan debt. In 1992, for example, the IRS withheld 720,326 refunds representing $530 million in student loan repayments. Since 1986 the IRS has offset 3,225,039 tax refunds, repaying over $2.1 billion in defaulted student loans.

Don't feel bad. You're not alone. According to a General Accounting Office report last year, hundreds of IRS employees had delinquent non-tax government debts such as students loans and child support payments. I wonder if they're offsetting their own tax refund checks? Hmmmm. Just wondering.

DEFAULTED STUDENT LOAN SOLUTIONS FOR TODAY'S CONSUMERS

Step 1: If you're being harassed by a debt collector about your student loan, take them out immediately. Use the strategies outlined in **BACK OFF!** to accomplish this goal. By eliminating the debt collector from the collection loop you will be able to deal with the original lender, or current note holder or loan servicer.

Step 2: Don't let the loan get all the way to the IRS stage. Negotiate, negotiate, negotiate. Communicate with the lender/servicer first and try to obtain a deferment. Some lenders will allow up to 3 years, usually ample time to get on your feet. These deferments will stop interest expense from accruing and keep consumers from being buried when they restart their repayment. Incidentally, borrowers have over a dozen deferment categories to qualify under, including the inability to find a job, poor health, service in the military or Peace Corps, or a desire to go back to school (and run up higher student loan balances!).

Step 3: Investigate the possibility of getting a student loan consolidation loan. This will extend the time it will take to repay your loan, but will allow you the chance to lower your interest rate and your payments, and most importantly, save your credit rating. A loan consolidator that fits into this category is Nellie Mae (New England Education Loan Marketing Corporation) at (800) 338-5626. If they cannot help you they may be able to refer you to someone in your part of the country.

Step 4: If you know your loan is in default, make the first move; contact the Department of Education at (800) 433-3243 and ask for their Credit Management and Debt Collection Services unit. Explain your situation, keep

detailed notes of people you talk to and when, and then follow up with a letter confirming your discussions. Be sure to
send this letter via certified mail so there are no mistakes. Use
the letter in Appendix U as your model for correspondence.

Step 5: If you have to deal with negative impact on your
credit bureau report from defaulting on a student loan used
to attend one of these "questionable" vocational institutions,
consider disputing this transaction with the credit bureaus.
Use the strategies outlined in this book and go after the
credit bureaus!

Step 6: Write to the Department of Education in
Washington, D.C. and tell them you need help! They really
do want to see borrowers get back into the system without
too much brain damage. They now understand that student
loan borrowers who are allowed to do this are not only grate-
ful, but also a positive impact on the economy. The
Department of Education will now reclassify your defaulted
student loan as current if you successfully make 12 consecutive payments. A second chance on your credit report? Yes!

Address your correspondence to:

U.S. Department of Education
7th & D Streets, Room 5102
Washington, D.C. 20202

Remember, *you have rights*. Senate investigations led by
Senator Sam Nunn [D-Ga.] revealed lenders that failed to
adhere to Department of Education guidelines. (Surprise!)

The Department of Education has failed to supervise over 10,000 primary lenders and 64 institutions operating in the secondary educational loan market. There are indications that 8 out of 10 lenders were not following proper DOE collection guidelines/procedures.

THIRTY-YEAR STUDENT LOAN REPAYMENT PERIODS?
A MAJOR BREAKTHROUGH!

As mentioned earlier in this chapter, the government has finally acknowledged that many student loan balances rival home mortgage balances in amount owed the lender, and has now created repayment schedules that extend up to 30 years.

Direct lending will be available through 104 schools during the first year of the new higher education financing program resulting from the Student Loan Reform Act enacted in August 1993. "Direct lending is user-friendly; the program makes borrowing simpler and more affordable," says Richard W. Riley, U.S. Secretary of Education. "This clearly marks a major milestone in reforming financial aid programs for students."

Approximately $1 billion in direct loans, or 5% of the total student loan volume, will be made during the program's inaugural year, 1994-95. By academic year 1998-99 direct loans will comprise at least 60% of total volume. Most importantly, students with other types of federal student loans may consolidate the loans and take advantage of a range of repayment options, including a plan tailored to the borrower's income.

Thanks to the Student Reform Act, students will now be able to receive loans through their schools and bypass private lenders. As a result of these and other changes, taxpayers should be saved an estimated $4.3 billion over five years. In addition, students with balances of $60,000 or more will be able to choose a 30-year repayment term, or make a fixed monthly payment for 10 years with another payment for an additional 12-30 years. Another option will allow the loan to be paid for 12 to 30 years at a monthly rate that varies with the loan balance, or monthly payments based on a percentage of income for up to 25 years.

Any way you look at it, our lawmakers and the Department of Education are finally waking up to the fact that yesterday's students sometimes need a fraction of the leniency that we extended to Chrysler back in the late 1970s when they were experiencing difficult times financially. (Compassion from our government? Legislators responding to our needs without the enticement of major campaign contributions? *What's going on here?*)

Take advantage of these programs before they change their minds! And make every penny count. After all, you could be paying it back for the next 30 years!

16

SECURED CREDIT CARDS: THE FIRST STEPS BACK

"It is the true nature of mankind to learn from mistakes, not from example."
–Fred Hoyle

MANY PEOPLE FEEL DISCOURAGED AND DEFEATED when they face credit problems. While the situation is serious, it is not hopeless, and certainly does not have to be permanent. With effort and commitment, consumers can restore their credit and go on to live comfortable, hassle-free financial lives. The following chapters explain how to rebuild your life after debt.

The term: "secured credit card" is really an oxymoron: the bank isn't really extending you credit; your credit line is usually in direct proportion to the amount of money you have on deposit with the issuing bank. Get it? A *"secured"* credit card. Who are the best candidates for these types of cards?

- People with poor credit

- Young people with no existing credit history

- "Newly single" individuals with no credit history of their own

- Self-employed people

- Immigrants with no U.S. credit history

- Retirees with assets but no income

Do you fit into one of these categories? Secured credit cards issued in 1992 jumped by 21% to 700,000. Not a surprising number when you consider that 60% of the applications for new credit cards were declined in 1992...that's over 10 million Americans who got the bad news that they couldn't qualify.

Insist on the following key points when you shop for a secured card as a rebuilding step:

- *No application fees.* It's getting competitive out there, so don't let anybody take advantage of you just because you aren't able to qualify for a conventional true credit card. There are plenty of banks that won't charge anything up front. Don't believe these ads that promise (for a fee) to deliver a credit card "regardless of credit history". In the majority of these cases consumers get nothing in return except another lesson in mail fraud.

- *Maximize the interest the issuing bank pays you for your deposit that secures your card.* It makes sense, doesn't it? The higher interest rate the bank is willing to pay you will offset the interest they'll charge you on any revolving balances you may run up. The difference is the net interest you'll be paying on your charges.

For example: Orchard Bank in Oregon carries no annual fees, charges 18.9% on your revolving balance, but pays you 5% for your deposit. The NET result is 13.9% for your "credit" line with no annual fee. For now it's the best deal in the country.

The flip side of the coin: There's a bank on the east coast that charges cardholders a $35 annual fee, and charges 18.99% on your charges but only pays 4% on your deposit. This net result comes out to 14.99% for your "credit" line plus another $35 a year just for the privilege of letting them take advantage of you.

I don't think so.

- *Make sure the bank you choose is FDIC insured.* There have been many cases of people desperate for a credit card making a substantial deposit and the issuing entity going broke. Remember: if it sounds too good to be true, it usually is.

- *Make sure the issuing bank will report your account activity to the major credit reporting bureaus.* It's not going to do you any good in your quest to rebuild your credit if nobody knows about it, right?

- *Find a bank that will let you graduate to a true credit card.* Many banks will offer "graduations" to unsecured credit cards after you have performed for a period of time, usually 18-24 months. (If you still have unpaid debts on your credit reports or a bankruptcy, this graduation process can be delayed a few years.) Performance simply means:

- *Keep within your card limits (the bank knows every*

time you use your card and also is alerted when you go over your limit).

- *Pay on time.* Keep on top of your bills this time around and pay the bank before the due date. Allow time for the mail...send your check at least 5 business days before the due date on the statement/invoice.

For a comprehensive list of banks offering these types of cards, contact the Bankcard Holders of America. They're located at 560 Herndon Parkway, Suite 120, Herndon, VA 22070. Here are two toll-free numbers to reach them: (800) 237-1800 or (800) 553-8025.

17

CONSUMER CREDIT COUNSELING SERVICE: WHOSE SIDE ARE THEY ON, ANYWAY?

"If you let other people do it for you, they will do it to you."
—Robert Anthony

IS IT JUST ME OR DOES ANYBODY ELSE OUT THERE get the least bit suspicious with all of this Consumer Credit Counseling Service (CCCS) hype?

Have you noticed on the bottom of your consumer credit report that there is a promotional/informational paragraph that touts the many wonders of CCCS? I want to know what they mean when they call CCCS a national, non-profit association.

I understand that the CCCS offices are sold like franchises around the country. They enjoy a brisk business helping consumers wade through their mess of debt, but at what price?

Once again, I asked Stephen Gardner about CCCS; recall that he is the former assistant Attorney General for the State of Texas and the man who initiated the lawsuit against TRW in 1991 (discussed in Chapter Two):

"I think that Consumer Credit Counseling Service is intrinsically deceptive. They're funded or incorporated by the very people they're truly representing... not the consumer/debtor but the creditors trying to collect the money.

I think they're a con; they pitch themselves as serving the consumer's best interest but they don't. Their promotions practices are deceptive and the consumers are being grossly misled.

If they were lawyers, they'd get disbarred! Representing one party and acting for the other? Come on! Think about it! If lawyers won't get involved in an enterprise like Consumer Credit Counseling, you know it must be bad."

Mr. Gardner's assessment of CCCS fits the picture that became clear while researching this book. Something that the good people at CCCS don't tell you is that they are paid by the creditors. That's right, the very people you owe money to are paying CCCS for the privilege of "helping" you through your debt problems.

Here's an example:

Suppose you owe ABC Department Store (among others) $1000 and CCCS assists you in negotiating a repayment schedule to your creditors. You are successful in repaying the entire $1000 through CCCS but in fact, only $875 is returned to the original creditor. A commission equal to 12.5% (in this case $125) is kept by CCCS for "helping" you through this period.

So whose interest is CCCS representing? The consumer's or the creditor's? Who is paying whom?

If you ask CCCS how they are paid, they will vaguely tell you that they receive a small fee from consumers, plus some funding from local banks and merchants. What they don't tell you is how that funding is derived, i.e. through commissions on the accounts they're servicing.

Furthermore, any notation showing up on your credit bureau reports that your account is being handled is far from favorable in the eyes of prospective lenders. What it tells a prospective lender is that you can't handle your debts.

In theory, CCCS is a good idea. Helping consumers repay their bills is wonderful...anything to keep them out of bankruptcy court. The problem is that CCCS does not make full disclosure to the consumer regarding how CCCS receives remuneration. In addition, in my opinion their reporting on your credit bureau report is a breach of your rights to privacy. Many prospective lenders look at a CCCS-notation as favorably as a Chapter 13 (bankruptcy wage-earner plan) filing.

CCCS doesn't have nice offices, extensive staffs, newspaper display advertising and radio/TV commercials because they're supposedly non-profit. However, they generate quite a bit of cash for their owners; moreover, creditors love them because they only have to pay a 12.5% commission to CCCS as opposed to as much as 50% to Vito's Knee Breaker Collection Agency.

<u>By the way:</u> I've talked to many, many consumers over the last 18 months who tried to work with CCCS and were rejected. CCCS suggested they file for bankruptcy. Wait a minute! I thought CCCS was there to help consumers avoid bankruptcy court.

Oh well.

Another one bites the dust.

18

THE CONSUMER'S CHECKLIST TOWARDS REBUILDING A LIFE AFTER DEBT

*"If the only tool you have is a hammer,
you tend to see every problem as a nail."*
–Abraham Maslow

IF YOU WORK THROUGH THIS CHECKLIST you will take positive, productive steps to rebuilding a strong credit rating. Don't get discouraged. Time, patience and persistence will pay off! Keep trying!

DO   **DON'T**

☑ Order current copies of all three major credit bureau reports. (Use the form letters in Appendices A and B)

☑ Carefully review reports. Look for erroneous information first.

☑ Make a copy of your reports. Do not write on the originals. Put these in your files. (Create a separate file for each credit bureau.)

☑ On your first pass at the credit bureau, circle all erroneous information on the copy of the corre-

DO   **DON'T**

sponding reports and return to them. Use your own variation of the cover letters provided in Appendices F and H.

☑ Address any excessive inquiries. Review Chapter XII and use the sample letters in Appendices M and N.

☑ Go after the "oldest and coldest" accounts listed. Use the strategies outlined in Chapter X.

☑ Circle any collection agency accounts and follow the instructions in Chapter X. Remember, the only way you may ultimately be able to get collection agency accounts off is through negotiations with the original creditor. Read on...

☑ For those accounts that are accurate, go directly to the original creditor and negotiate a deal. Follow the directions outlined in Chapter X and hang tough. When they agree, get them to sign a letter agreeing to the terms you've negotiated before you send them any money. (Refer to the sample letter in Appendix G)

☑ Start rebuilding your credit through secured credit cards. Refer to Chapter XVII and call for a list of banks offering best secured card deals.

☑ Read through the resources list located in Appendix BB to see what associations or companies you need to contact to begin your journey back to the credit mainstream.

DO   DON'T

☑ Whatever you do, do not pay any creditor unless they agree to remove the negative information! Otherwise you will restart the credit reporting clock and extend your misery for another 7 years from the date of your last payment!

Don't pay a "credit clinic" to fix your credit. At this ☑ stage of the game, you have more insight from reading this book than they do...and you've spent far less than they'll try to charge you!

Don't fall for these scams that offer (for a prepaid ☑ fee) to issue you a credit card. Regardless of credit history. Remember, if it sounds too good to be true, it usually is.

Don't fall for the "pre-approved Gold Card" scam. ☑ The fee is normally in the $30-50 range and you get exactly what they offer... a card that is plastic, and colored gold. Their catalog that you can use your "gold card" for is full of overpriced junk. Remember, if it sounds too good to be true, it usually is.

Don't get discouraged. Time, patience, persistence and your new knowledge will pay big benefits!

Keep trying!

19

THE FINAL STRAW: COMPLAIN TO THE FTC

*"Great works are performed
not by strength but by perseverance."*
–Samuel Johnson

DO YOU REMEMBER THE CLASS-ACTION LAWSUIT I talked about earlier in the book that was initiated by the State of Texas' Attorney General?

That suit was a direct result of consumer complaints.

If consumers across America fail to speak up and voice their displeasure with the system, we are all sentenced to live within a system that's broken.

You've got no excuse for not writing! Appendix Z offers a list of all of the regional Federal Trade Commission offices. For your convenience, Appendix S furnishes a model complaint letter to the FTC. Use the same letter format to complain to your state's attorney general. Use it.

And more importantly, follow-up when you receive the FTC's standard complaint forms. Follow up, document your complaint and push them to the point of resolution. If you don't make your voice heard, you've just wasted your money on this book. Or maybe not...give it to a friend for their birthday.

As a result of the suit against TRW, TRW is now giving *every* American a free copy of their credit bureau report once a year, just for asking. How will you ever know if there is erroneous information on your credit report if you don't have a chance to get a look at it? Well here's your chance.

Revised in January '93, the new friendlier TRW consumer credit report format is another direct result of the lawsuit initiated by the AG of Texas—an action that was started by letters complaining about the unfairness and inaccuracies to which consumers were being subjected.

Remember America: no matter what the problem, the squeaky wheel always gets the grease.

Ultimately, it's up to you to take control and begin rebuilding your *Life After Debt!*

20

CLOSING THOUGHTS TO AMERICA'S POLICY MAKERS AND TAKERS

"Power without a nation's confidence is nothing."
–Catherine the Great

EVERY SYSTEM HAS ITS GOOD POINTS AND CORRESPONDING DRAW-BACKS. No matter how hard we try to invent a "better mouse-trap" there will always be that probable margin of error.

Ralph Nader surfaced in the 1960's to become the protector of the American consumer. Big business took an instant dislike to him, but through his efforts the quality of American life has improved.

Safety is now in the front of the public conscience. Defective cars are recalled, pricing discrimination against women is more than just a running gag, and Americans are more aware of their rights under federal laws. Many of these laws have been on the books for years, but until recently, average consumers had no clue of how to use these laws to protect themselves.

Let's see: the 1980's brought us phrases like "hostile take-over" and "junk bonds" and "high tech" and "cutting edge."

The 1990's are developing into the "politically correct" decade, with a heavy emphasis of "empowerment."

Empowerment is what this book is all about.

It's not about screwing the credit system; it's screwed up just fine on its own, thank you.

It's not about defrauding creditors. It's not about cooking the books in hopes of evading the latest tax plan out of Washington that promises to save America's financial future.

Life After Debt is all about understanding the laws that are in force today.

It's about playing with the hand we're dealt and making the best of it. In order to benefit from the current system, we must understand the system and its inherent strengths and weaknesses.

Our nation's lawmakers **are** responding: the champions of the consumer in the area of credit data includes people like Rep. Joseph P. Kennedy II (D-Mass.), Rep. Esteban Torres (D-Calif.), Sen. Richard H. Bryan (D-Nev.), Sen. Christopher S. Bond (R-Mo.), Sen. Donald Riegle (D-Mich.) and Rep. Henry Gonzalez (D-Texas). These lawmakers intend to level the playing field of credit information. Naturally, they are met with a barrage of warnings from lobby groups including the Associated Credit Bureaus, the American Collectors Association and the American Bankers Association. I have faith that the champions will persevere.

Everybody is pointing their fingers at each other and whipping out statistics that prove their points. You know the saying, "Figures don't lie, but liars can figure"? Anybody can get any expert to come up with any set of statistics that favors their cause and present these to the jury. Unfortunately our system is built more upon the theory of "my lawyer can beat up your lawyer" than on the truth, or on the facts.

Every consumer needs to remember these facts:

1. Collection agencies and erroneous credit reports are the largest source of complaints to the Federal Trade Commission.

2. Everybody in this country depends on their credit history at some point in their life. Even not having a credit history is, in effect, having a history.

3. We are all tattooed from birth to death with those nine digits that bare the misleading title of "social security number." This is nothing more than an inventory number for the IRS, credit bureaus, health insurance companies and other collectors of information to label us with for positive identification. And herein lies the problem.....

If this information is not correct, we're doomed. Our ability to get a better job, to buy a new car, a new home, to generally improve our quality of life ultimately revolves around the information contained in a file under this nine digit number.

Today we are able to view our credit files and challenge or dispute the validity of information contained in these files. However those national purveyors of data, the giants of the information industry known as TRW, Equifax and Trans Union continue to find new ways to create profits from information about you and me. Personal information that is nobody's business is finding its way into these new "Consumer Reports" that not only combine our paying and buying habits, but integrate our medical histories...including physical ailments, medications and psychological counseling histories.

I can see it now: a new "gold" charge card targeted at manic depressives who drive foreign cars and are currently taking lithium.

The laws that are currently in force are satisfactory at best...but they're just a starting point. Most of the "consumer protection" laws were drafted in the 1970's and updated from time to time since then. They became law long before the information explosion of the 1980's and 90's. Unfortunately, many consumers are unaware of these laws because very little effort or money went into promoting them. Gee. I wonder why!?

Think about those innocuous little bar codes on every item you purchase at the grocery store. That information about what you buy and how often you buy it must be compiled somewhere, don't you think? If you pay with a credit card, they can link that product purchasing information directly to you. If you use a check, they can link it to your driver's license number or your checking account number. Is nothing sacred? Is this sounding paranoid once again?

I don't think so.

Don't think for one minute that there isn't one helluva database out there being built with everything anyone ever wanted to know about you...whether you like it or not.

If these companies have the right to collect all of this information on us, then we must have access to any information contained about ourselves in those data banks. We must have access to not only credit reports under the Fair Credit Reporting Act, but any database in the country that is collecting and reselling information about each of us.

After all, if these corporations are able to make a nice profit on this information about all of us, shouldn't we have the right to inspect this information to make sure it is indeed, truthful, complete and correct?

Our nation's lenders have a right to gather the information necessary to make the best lending decision. I recognize their need to gain as much pertinent data and insight to reduce their chance of borrower defaults. This is a nation built on credit, but now the foundation has been replaced with information.

This information must be accurate to protect all parties. But as I've illustrated, it is, unfortunately, an imperfect system that is too accessible by too many people. There are not enough paper trails, not enough checks and balances, and not enough informed consumers to insure that you can enjoy a *Life After Debt*...

Until now.

Appendix A

Sample Letter to Obtain Free Annual TRW Credit Report

Appendix B

Sample Letter To Obtain
Equifax/Trans Union Credit Report

ROBERT PETRIE
2244 Morning Glory Road
New Rochelle, NJ 07662

September 7, 1993

Equifax Credit
P.O. Box 740241
Atlanta, GA 30374-0241

RE: Copy of my credit report

To Whom It May Concern:

Please forward a current copy of my credit report to my address listed above.

My date of birth is: 10-03-61.

My social security number is: 319-88-0000.

Enclosed is a money order in the amount of $8.00 to cover the associated costs.

Thank you for your prompt assistance in this matter.

Sincerely,

Robert Petrie

RP:sr

Appendix C

Sample Letter to Obtain Copy of Credit
Bureau Report After Denial Extension

WALTER O'REILEY
Rural Route 3, Box 1A
Ottumwa, IA 52501

September 19, 1993

TransUnion Corporation
P.O. Box 7000
North Olmstead, OH 44070

RE: Free copy of my credit report due to denial of credit by Twin Falls Furniture
Store

To Whom It May Concern:
Please forward a free current copy of my credit report to my address listed above.

My date of birth is: 09-17-93.

My social security number is: 482-00-0000.

I was denied credit by Twin Falls Furniture Store based on information contained
in a credit report they obtained from your company. Under rules covered by the
Fair Credit Reporting Act, please let this letter serve as my official request for
this report.

I enclosed a copy of my current driver's license to verify my identity.

Thank you for your prompt assistance in this matter.

Sincerely,

Walter O'Reilly

WGO:wgo

HOW TO SEND CERTIFIED MAIL

Using U.S. Postal Service Form #3800

Step One: Fill in the first line (a) with the name of the Collection Agency.

Step Two: Fill in the second line (b) with the street or mailing address of the Collection Agency.

Step Three: Fill in the third line (c) with the city, state and zip code of the Collection Agency.

Step Four: Moisten the green label (bottom half) of the form and attach directly to the right of your return address (making sure you do not cover your return address).

The Post Office will fill out the rest of the form after you have paid them the appropriate fee.

U.S. Postal Service Form #3800

- EXAMPLE -

```
P 882 597 882

Certified Mail Receipt
No Insurance Coverage Provided
Do not use for International Mail
(See Reverse)

ABC Collection Agency
P.O. Box 12345
New York, NY 10010-12345

Postage          $
Certified Fee
Special Delivery Fee
Restricted Delivery Fee
Return Receipt Showing
to Whom & Date Delivered
Return Receipt Showing to Whom,
Date, & Address of Delivery
TOTAL Postage   $
& Fees
Postmark or Date

PS Form 3800, June 1990

Fold at line over top of envelope to the
right of the return address.

CERTIFIED
P 882 597 882
MAIL
```

U.S. Post Office Form #3811
(Green Return Reply/Receipt Card)

Step One: Fill in your complete address (a)

Step Two: In section 3, fill in the name of the Collection Agency and name of the representative to which your letter is addressed. Be sure to include their zip code.

Step Three: In section 4a, fill in the number from U.S. Post Office Form #3800 (refer to Appendix D). Remember, this number should also be printed across the top of the letter being sent to the Collection Agency and representative.

Step Four: In section 4b, mark the box with the word "Certified" next to it.

All of the other lines should be left blank. They will be filled in by the mail carrier delivering the letter to the Collection Agency and representative.

Appendix E

U.S. Post Office Form #3811-A
(Yellow Reply Card Tracer)

This card is only filled out when it is apparent your green reply receipt card has been lost. Be sure to allow 14 days for the return of the green card.

Be sure to have all of your receipts from when you originally mailed the letter. You should have attached to your file copy of the letter you mailed the white half of U.S. Post Office Form #3800. When you mailed your letter, the Post Office filled in this part of the form, showing which services you requested and paid for, along with their postmark. This will give the postal clerk ample evidence to send this yellow tracer card through the system.

Step One: Fill in your name and the same mailing/return address you wrote on the green card (a).

Step Two: Fill in your city, state and zip code on this line (b). This will make sure this card is returned to your post office branch.

129

Step Three: Fill in the date you mailed your original letter on line 3. Use the date of the postmark on the white half of U.S. Postal Service Form #3800.

Step Four: Fill in the "Certified No." of the letter you originally mailed on line 6. This number will be the same one printed at the top of the white half of U.S. Postal Service Form #3800 (referred to above).

Step Five: Fill in the name and address of the Collection Agency where you sent your original letter on line 9. This name and address should match the one written on the white half of U.S. Postal Service Form #3800.

The postal clerk will handle the rest of the lines. You should receive this card within 14 days from the date you put in the tracer card.

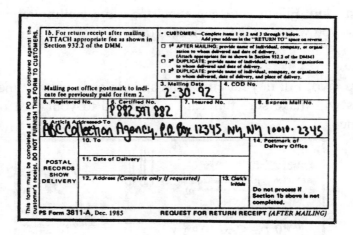

Appendix F

Sample Letter Format Utilized to Remove Old Report Entries

EDWARD BAXTER
3300 Twin Cities Tower, Apt. 2000
Minneapolis, MN 55440

September 3, 1993

TransUnion Corporation
P.O. Box 7000
North Olmstead, OH 44070

RE: Removal of old/outdated information

To Whom It May Concern:

I received my recent Trans Union credit report you sent and I need to bring to your attention several entries that are outdated.

1) The entry from St. Paul Medical Center showing date of last activity of August 1, 1986 needs to be removed;

2) The entry from Minneapolis Ambulance Company dated August 1, 1986 also needs to be removed.

Since both entries are more than seven years old, under the Fair Credit Reporting Act, these must be removed. Please send my updated/revised credit report to me after these have been deleted.

Thank you for your attention to this matter.

Sincerely,

Edward Baxter

EB:mr

Appendix G

Sample Letter Format Utilized To Settle An Outstanding Balance With A Creditor

MR. WARD CLEAVER
211 Pine Street
Mayfield, NY 12117

<u>**VIA CERTIFIED MAIL, RETURN RECEIPT REQUESTED #P 123 456 789**</u>

February 30, 1994

Mr. Richard Head
Vice President of Financial Services
ACME Department Store
1234 Disk Drive
Sonoffa Beach, CA 90010-1234

RE: Agreed settlement of outstanding balance of $725.00 on account #123-456

Dear Mr. Head:

As we have discussed via telephone on several occasions over the last few months, I am willing to settle the outstanding balance on my account referenced above.

By affixing your signature on this letter of settlement/agreement, you agree on behalf of ACME Department Stores, Inc. to the following:

1) You agree to accept a total of $72.50 as an agreed settlement of all outstanding charges/fees on the account referenced above. This will be paid to your company in certified funds as soon as I receive a signed and dated copy of this letter from you;

2) You agree to cease any and all attempts to collect this debt, either directly or through a Collection Agency;

– continued –

Mr. Richard Head, *ACME Department Store*   **Page 2**
February 30, 1994

3) You agree not to sell this debt to any third party since you now recognize this account to be "SETTLED AS AGREED";

4) You agree to retract **all** negative or derogatory remarks you may have reported on my credit report with any credit reporting agency located in the United States.

This agreement will not be binding until I receive a signed/dated original of this letter from you and in turn, I remit certified funds to your company thus closing this transaction.

Please sign and return a copy of the letter enclosed in the attached pre-addressed/postage paid envelope.

Thank you for your cooperation in this matter.

Sincerely,   **ACCEPTED AND AGREED TO:**

_____

Ward Cleaver   Richard Head   Date

WC:bs

Appendix H

**Sample Letter To Dispute Negative Credit Report
Entries From Phantom/Non-Existing Companies**

ROBERT EWING
Southfork Ranch
Braddock, TX 75200

May 3, 1993

TRW National Consumer Relations Center
P.O. Box 749029
Dallas, TX 75374-9029

RE: Negative entry reported by RepublicBank/Texas

To Whom It May Concern:

According to my latest credit report from TRW, I have a negative entry
being reported by:

RepublicBank/Texas
Amount charged off: $1,500,000
Date charged off: 04/31/87

Please remove this entry at once.

Sincerely,

Robert Ewing

RE:sl

Appendix I

Sample Letter To Current Card Company Closing Account In Anticipation Of Separation/Divorce Proceedings

DR. LILITH STERNIN
19 Lourdes Avenue, #1
Boston, MA 02130

VIA CERTIFIED MAIL, RETURN RECEIPT REQUESTED #P 123 456 789

May 20, 1993

American Express Travel Related Services Company, Inc.
Credit Bureau Unit
P.O. Box 7871
Ft. Lauderdale, FL 33329-7871

RE: Account #3728-000000-00000

To Whom It May Concern:

Please let this letter serve as my official request to close my account referenced above.

I am about to file for divorce from my husband, Dr. Frasier Crane and would like him removed from my account at this time to prevent any unauthorized charges.

At this time I would appreciate your opening a new account in my name only and sending the new card to my new mailing address:
P.O. Box 93082
Boston, MA 02130

Thank you for your prompt attention to this matter.

Sincerely,

Dr. Lilith Sternin

LS:rh

Appendix J

Sample Letter Requesting The Release Of Spouse From Automobile Loan/Lease Note

HENRY MITCHELL
4505 Elm Street
Hillsdale, CA 95666

<u>**VIA CERTIFIED MAIL, RETURN RECEIPT REQUESTED #P 123 456 789**</u>

September 22, 1993

Mr. P. Hart
Credit Manager, General Motors Acceptance Corporation
P.O. Box 1000
San Francisco, CA 94000

RE: Note #3M-TA3

Dear Mr. Hart:

Please let this letter serve as my official request of GMAC to release my wife, Alice Mitchell from the note referenced above.

We are in the middle of finalizing our divorce and part of the terms of agreement includes my getting her released from any potential/contingent liability on this note.

My credit report and payment record should reflect my good standing and stability with GMAC and warrant this release. If you should require an updated financial statement for your files, please let me know.

I need to get this situation handled as soon as possible. I look forward to your prompt reply.

Sincerely,

Henry Mitchell

HM:ka

Appendix K

Sample Letter Requesting The Release Of Spouse From Home Mortgage Note

ARCHIBALD BUNKER
704 Houser Street
Queens, NY 10011

VIA CERTIFIED MAIL, RETURN RECEIPT REQUESTED #P 123 456 789

January 12, 1993

Mr. Frank Lorenzo
Vice President, Flushing Mortgage Company
P.O. Box 1991
Flushing, NY 10010

RE: Account #987-654

Dear Mr. Lorenzo:

Please let this letter serve as my official request of Flushing Mortgage Company to release my wife, Edith, from the note referenced above.

We are in the middle of finalizing our divorce and part of the terms of agreement includes my getting her released from any potential/contingent liability on this note.

My credit report and payment record should reflect my good standing and stability with Flushing Mortgage and warrant this release. If you should require an updated financial statement for your files, please let me know.

I need to get this situation handled as soon as possible. I look forward to your prompt reply.

Sincerely,

Archibald Bunker

AB:gs

Appendix L

Sample Letter To Credit Bureau Requesting Removal Of Negative Information From Former Spouse

MILBURN DRYSDALE
Commerce Bank of Beverly Hills
3300 Sunset Blvd.
Beverly Hills, CA 90010

<u>**VIA CERTIFIED MAIL, RETURN RECEIPT REQUESTED #P 123 456 789**</u>

September 7, 1993

Citibank
ATTN: Mrs. Winnie Gillis
Bankcard Collections
1030 Broad St.
Shrewsbury, NJ 07702

RE: Account #4129 000000 000000

Dear Mrs. Gillis:

After examining my current TRW, Equifax and Trans Union credit bureau reports, it has come to my attention that your bank has mistakenly recorded the payment history/ liability for the account referenced above.

This account belongs to my ex-wife, Margaret Drysdale and is her sole responsibility. We have been divorced for the last 4 years and I have never used this account.

You have 30 days from the date of receipt of this letter to remove all information from all credit bureaus carrying this information in my credit records, or prove to me in writing that I have ever signed any documentation taking responsibility for this account.

My social security number is: 545-99-0000.

I look forward to your prompt response.

Sincerely,

Milburn Drysdale

MD:jh

Appendix M

**Sample Letter To Credit Bureau
Requesting Reserach Of Unknown Inquiries**

BERNARD M. FIFE
411 Elm Street
Mayberry, NC 27611

October 3, 1993

Trans Union Corporation
P.O. Box 7000
North Olmstead, OH 44070

RE: Unexplained inquiries on my credit report

To Whom It May Concern:

After examining my Trans Union credit report, I noticed two inquiries at the bottom of the page that I would like you to document or remove:

1) Mount Pilot Motors, Mt. Pilot, NC;
2) Pierre's Men's Store, Raleigh, NC.

I have never applied for credit with either one of these companies and request that you investigate these notations.

I look forward to your prompt reply.

Sincerely,

Bernard M. Fife

BMF:oc

Appendix N

Sample Letter To Credit Bureau
Challenging Validity Of Inquiry/Demanding Removal

BERNARD M. FIFE
411 Elm Street
Mayberry, NC 27611

<u>**VIA CERTIFIED MAIL, RETURN RECEIPT REQUESTED #P 123 456 789**</u>

October 3, 1993

Trans Union Corporation
P.O. Box 7000
North Olmstead, OH 44070

RE: Immediate removal of unexplained inquiries on my credit report

To Whom It May Concern:

My Trans Union credit report contains two inquiries that are unauthorized and hereby demand their removal at once:

1) Mount Pilot Motors, Mt. Pilot, NC;
2) Pierre's Men's Store, Raleigh, NC.

I have never applied for credit with either one of these companies and request that you document both or remove at once.

I am requesting a copy of my signature on a credit application to either of these companies or a copy of my written authorization allowing them to examine my credit report.

According to the Fair Credit Reporting Act these inquiries must be documented or removed.

You have 30 days from receipt of this letter to verify this information. I look forward to your reply with a copy of my updated and revised report.

Sincerely,

Bernard M. Fife

BMF:oc

Appendix O

STEVE DOUGLAS
837 Mill St.
Bryan Park, OH 43216

August 24, 1993

Trans Union Corporation
P.O. Box 7000
North Olmstead, OH 44070

To Whom It May Concern:

After examining my recent Trans Union credit report, I noticed the following notation:

VITO'S COLLECTION AGENCY $1,972.00

This is <u>not</u> mine.

Please remove <u>immediately.</u>

Sincerely,

Steve Douglas

SD:bhd

Appendix P

Sample Letter To Resturcture Balance Owed To Hospital/Health Care Provider

ALFRED DELVECCHIO
7799 Haley Way
Milwaukee, WI 53201

<u>**VIA CERTIFIED MAIL, RETURN RECEIPT REQUESTED #P 123 456 789**</u>

January 15, 1993

Mr. Warren Weber
Chairman, Milwaukee General Hospital
2000 Cunningham Blvd.
Milwaukee, WI 53210

RE: Account #654-321, balance owed: $1984.00

Dear Mr. Weber:

My insurance company has paid what it owes your hospital and I owe the balance on the account referenced above.

I fully intend to pay this balance in full but need your hospital's cooperation in restructuring the payment plan your accounting office has proposed.

I'm unable to make the minimum payments your hospital has requested but can make payments in the amount of $50 a month for the next 12 months. I am on a restricted income due to my recent illness and cannot pay any more than this at this time. Your account representatives have made it clear that they intend to refer my account to a collection agency.

I will not deal with a debt collector, Mr. Weber. I have been making my payment intentions clear to your hospital and cannot improve this plan at this time. Harassment at the hands of a debt collector will only irritate the situation and diminish my ability or desire to repay any balance owed to your hospital.

Please contact me in writing at once so that we can work out terms that are acceptable to all parties involved.

Thank you for your prompt attention to this matter.

Sincerely,

Alfred Delvecchio

AF:ca

Sample Letter Confirming Renotiated Repayment Terms
For Balance Owed To Hospital/Health Care Provider

ALFRED DELVECCHIO
7799 Haley Way
Milwaukee, WI 53201

VIA CERTIFIED MAIL, RETURN RECEIPT REQUESTED #P 123 456 789

March 15, 1993

Mr. Warren Weber
Chairman, Milwaukee General Hospital
2000 Cunningham Blvd.
Milwaukee, WI 55555

RE: Account #654-321, balance owed: $1984.00

Dear Mr. Weber:

Thank you for your recent letter about my account referenced above.

I appreciate your willingness to work with me to restructure the repayment of the balance I owe to Milwaukee General Hospital. By working out new terms with me we have both avoided dealing with a collection agency...your hospital get 100 cents on the dollar and I don't have to be harassed.

I will forward my first payment of $50 when I receive the original of this letter with your signature at the bottom accepting the following terms:

1) Twelve monthly payments in the amount of $50 each followed by
2) Twelve additional monthly payments in the amount of $115.33 each.
3) You agree not to report any negative information about this account to any credit reporting bureau in the United States as long as I make my payments as agreed.

– continued –

Mr. Warren Webber   Page 2
March 15, 1993

By signing your name in the space provided below, you hereby agree to
the terms and conditions outlined herein.

Sincerely,   **AGREED AND ACCEPTED**

_____

Alfred Delvecchio   Warren Weber   Date
                                     Chairman, Milwaukee General Hospital
AD:rc

Appendix R

Sample Letter To Physician Challenging Fees Charged

Ernest T. Douglas
8868 Camino Real Drive
Sherman Oaks, CA 90010

VIA CERTIFIED MAIL, RETURN RECEIPT REQUESTED #P 123 456 789

September 19, 1993

Dr. David Zorba
County General Hospital
Los Angeles, CA 90010

RE: Your account #765-321-A, balance $198.00

Dear Dr. Zorba:

My insurance company has paid what it deems appropriate for your services rendered under the industry-accepted "USUAL & CUSTOMARY" standards.

I have checked with several other doctors in your market area and the local medical association, in addition to consulting with my insurance carrier about your fees charged. It is apparent that your fees are appreciably higher for the procedures you performed and I hereby request that you document/justify this charge.

If you cannot justify these higher fees then let this letter serve as your official notice of my intent to refuse any further payment on this account. Furthermore, if you attempt any collection activity that may include referring my account to a third party debt collector or placing any negative information on my credit bureau reports, I will file suit against you.

I do not have a problem in paying my bills that are rightfully owed but I refuse to pay for charges that are unreasonable.

I look forward to your reply.

Sincerely,

Ernest T. Douglas

ETD:ms

Appendix S

CHIN HO KELLY
2565 Mauna Kea Place
Honolulu, HI 96820

April 26, 1993

Federal Trade Commission
450 Golden Gate Avenue, Room 12470
San Francisco, CA 94102

To Whom It May Concern:

I am having difficulties with several companies and request that you immediately send to me all of the appropriate forms to file complaints with your agency about the violations of the following two federal laws:

> The Fair Debt Collections Practices Act
> The Fair Credit Reporting Act

I look forward to your prompt reply.

Sincerely,

Chin Ho Kelly

CHK:gf

Appendix T

Demand Letter To Credit Bureau To Remove Incorrect Information

ALFRED PENNYWORTH
1 Wayne Manor
Gotham City, NY 10040

VIA CERTIFIED MAIL. RETURN RECEIPT REQUESTED #P 000 000 000

January 12, 1993

TRW National Consumer Relations Center
P.O. Box 749029
Dallas, TX 75374-9029

To Whom It May Concern:

Please let this letter serve as your official written notice that you have thirty (30) days from your receipt of this letter to remove the following entry:

AMERICAN EXPRESS Acct. #3724 000000 00000 Charge Off 3/90

This is not my account, and never has been; you are destroying my reputation in the credit community. If you do not remove this immediately, I intend to file a complaint with the Federal Trade Commission and the state Attorney General's office, in addition to seeking any and all legal remedies available to me by law.

GIVE THIS MATTER THE ATTENTION IT DESERVES AND CORRECT THIS SITUATION AT ONCE.

I look forward to receiving a corrected copy of my credit report with your response.

Sincerely,

Alfred Pennyworth

AF:hc

Appendix U

Blank Letter For Corresponding To Department of Education

_____
_____
_____

__VIA CERTIFIED MAIL, RETURN RECEIPT REQUESTED # _____

Date: _____

U.S. Department of Education
ATTN: Student Loan Workouts
7th and D Streets, Room 5102
Washington, D.C. 20202

RE: Account # _____

To Whom It May Concern:

I need to restructure my outstanding student loan (my account number is referenced above).

It is my understanding that under the Student Loan Reform Act (Public Law 103-66) there are several options available to me. I wish to get this situation restructured and under control as soon as possible.

Please forward all applications and paperwork to my attention at the address listed at the top of this page, as soon as possible. I wish to establish a repayment plan immediately.

Sincerely,

_____

Opie Taylor   Page 2
March 16, 1993

"Miss Edwards" proposed that I make payments in the amount of
$374 a month. I countered with the following terms:

1) I can make payments in the amount of $100 a month;

2) Before I enter into this repayment agreement, I must get the
following agreement (enclosed) signed by a duly-authorized
representative of your organization, agreeing not to report this loan in
a negative manner on any credit bureau in the United States.

No wonder debt collectors have such a bad reputation; Miss Edwards'
performance was anything but professional or constructive.

I cannot be plagued by negative comments on my credit report(s) for
seven years after I repay this debt, and must have signed assurances
from your organization guaranteeing me this will not happen.

I look forward to your reply.

Sincerely,

Opie Taylor

OP:bt

Appendix V

Sample Letter To Hospital
Requesting An Audit Of Account

TIM O'HARA
2211 Laurel Canyon Road, Apt. B
Los Angeles, CA 90010

September 4, 1993

Los Angeles Memorial Hospital
ATTN: Accounting Supervisor
3300 Lankershim Blvd.
Los Angeles, CA 90000

RE: Account #654-987-123

To Whom It May Concern:

Please let this letter serve as my official request for a complete and comprehensive audit of my account referenced above.

I am trying to reconcile all of the charges with my insurance carrier and require all of this information as soon as possible.

Please forward this information to my address listed above.

Sincerely,

Tim O'Hara

TO:um

THE FAIR CREDIT REPORTING ACT

Public Law #91-508, Title VI
as amended by Public law #95-598

TITLE VI - PROVISIONS RELATING TO CREDIT REPORTING AGENCIES

AMENDMENT OF CONSUMER CREDIT PROTECTION ACT

Sec. 601. The consumer credit Protection Act is amended by adding at the end thereof the following new title:

Title VI - Consumer Credit Reporting

"Sec.
"601. Short title.
"602. Findings and purpose.
"603. Definitions and rules of construction.
"604. Permissible purposes of reports.
"605. Obsolete information.
"606. Disclosure of investigative consumer reports.
"607. Compliance procedures.
"608. Disclosures to governmental agencies.
"609. Disclosure to consumers.
"610. Conditions of disclosure to consumers.
"611. Procedure in case of disputed accuracy.

"612. Charges for certain disclosures.

"613. Public record information for employment purposes.

"614. Restrictions on investigative consumer reports.

"615. Restrictions on investigative consumer reports.

"616. Civil liability for willful noncompliance.

"618. Jurisdiction of courts;limitation of actions.

"619. Obtaining information under false pretenses.

"620. Unauthorized disclosures by officers or employees.

"621. Administrative enforcement.

"622. Relation to State laws.

"§Short title

"This title may be cited as the Fair Credit Reporting Act.

"§602. Findings and purpose

"(a) The Congress makes the following findings:

"(1) The banking system is dependent upon fair and accurate credit reporting. Inaccurate credit reports directly impair the efficiency of the banking system, and unfair credit reporting methods undermine the public confidence which is essential to the continued functioning of the banking system.

"(2) An elaborate mechanism has been developed for investigating and evaluating the credit worthiness, credit standing, credit capacity, character, and general reputation of consumers.

"(3) Consumer reporting agencies have assumed a vital role in assembling and evaluating consumer credit and other information on consumers.

"(4) There is a need to insure that consumer reporting agencies exercise their grave responsibilities with fairness, impartiality, and a respect for the consumer's right to privacy.

"(b) It is the purpose of this title to require that consumer reporting agencies adopt reasonable procedures for meeting the needs of commerce for consumer credit, personnel, insurance, and other information in a manner which is fair and equitable to the consumer, with regard to the confidentiality, accuracy, relevancy, and proper utilization of such information in accordance with the requirements of this title.

"§603. Definitions and rules of construction

"(a) Definitions and rules of construction set forth in this section are applicable for the purposes of this title.

"(b) The term 'person' means any individual, partnership, corporation, trust, estate, cooperative, association, government or governmental subdivision or agency, or other entity.

"(c) The term 'consumer' means an individual.

"(d) The term 'consumer report means any written, oral, or other communication of any information by a consumer reporting agency bearing on a consumer;s credit worthiness, credit standing, credit capacity, character, general reputation, personal characteristics, or mode of living which is used or expected to be used or collected in whole or in part for the purpose of serving as a factor in establishing the consumer's eligibility for (1) credit or insurance to be used primarily for personal, family, or household purposes, or (2) employment purposes, or (3) other purposes authorized under section 604. The term does not include (A) any report containing information solely as to transactions or experiences between the consumer and the person making the report; (B) any authorization or approval of a specific extension of credit directly or indirectly by the issuer of a credit card or similar device; or (C) any report in which a person who has been requested by a third party to make a specific extension of credit directly or indirectly to a consumer conveys his decision with respect to such request, if the third party advises the consumer of the name and address of the person to whom the request was made and such person makes the disclosures to the consumer required under section 615.

"(e) The term 'investigative consumer report' means a consumer report or portion thereof in which information on a consumer's character, general reputation, personal characteristics, or mode of living is obtained through personal interviews with neighbors, friends, or associates of the consumer reported on or with others with whom he is acquainted or who may have knowledge concerning any such items of information. However, such information shall not include specific factual information on a consumer's credit record obtained directly from a creditor of the consumer of from a consumer reporting agency when such information was obtained directly from a creditor of the consumer or from the consumer.

"(f) The term 'consumer reporting agency' means any person which, for monetary fees, dues, or on a cooperative nonprofit basis, regularly engages in whole or in part in the practice of assembling or evaluating consumer credit information or other information on consumers for the purpose of furnishing consumer reports to third parties, and which uses any means or facility or interstate commerce for the purpose of preparing or furnishing consumer reports.

"(g) The term 'file', when used in connection with information on any consumer, means all of the information on that consumer recorded and retained by a consumer reporting agency regardless of how the information is stored.

"(h) The term 'employment purposes' when used in connection with a consumer report means a report used for the purpose of evaluating a consumer for employment, promotion, reassignment or retention as an employee.

"(i) The term 'medical information' means information or records obtained, with the consent of the individual to whom it relates, from licensed physicians or medical practitioners, hospitals, clinics, or other medical or medically related facilities.

"§604. Permissible purposes of reports

"A consumer reporting agency may furnish a consumer report under the following circumstances and no other:

"(1) In response to the order of a court having jurisdiction to issue such an order.

"(2) In accordance with the written instructions of the consumer to whom it relates.

"(3) To a person which it has reason to believe—

"(A) intends to use the information in connection with a credit transaction involving the consumer on whom the information is to be furnished and involving the extension of credit to, or review or collection of an account of, the consumer; or

"(B) intends to use the information for employment purposes; or

"(C) intends to use the information in connection with the underwriting of insurance involving the consumer; or

"(D) intends to use the information in connection with a determination of the consumer's eligibility for license or other benefit granted by a governmental instrumentality required by law to consider an applicant's financial responsibility or status; or

"(E) other wise has a legitimate business need for the information in connection with a business transaction involving the consumer.

"§605. Obsolete information

"(a) Except as authorized under subsection (b), no consumer reporting agency may make any consumer report containing any of the following items of information:

"(1) Cases under title 11 of the United States Code or under the Bankruptcy Act that, from the date of entry of the order for relief or the date of adjudication, as the case may be, antedate the report by more than 10 years.

"(2) Suits and judgments which, from date of entry, antedate the report by more than seven years or until the governing statute of limitations has expired, whichever is the longer period.

"(3) Paid tax liens which, from date of payment, antedate the report by more than seven years.

"(4) Accounts placed for collection or charged to profit and loss which antedate the report by more than seven years.

"(5) Records of arrest, indictment, or conviction of crime which, from date of disposition, release, or parole, antedate the report by more than seven years.

"(6) Any other adverse item of information which antedates the report by more than seven years.

"(b) Any other adverse item of information which antedates the report by more than seven years.

"b) The provisions of subsection (a) are not applicable in the case of any consumer credit report to be used in connection with—

"(1) a credit transaction involving, or which may reasonably be expected to involve, a principal amount of $50,000 or more;

"(2) the underwriting of life insurance involving, or which may reasonable be expected to involve, a face amount of $50,000 or more; or"(3) the employment of any individual at an annual salary which equals, or which may reasonably be expected to equal $20,000 or more.

"§606. Disclosure of investigative consumer reports

"(a) A person may not procure or cause to be prepared an investigative consumer report on any consumer unless—

"(1) it is clearly and accurately disclosed to the consumer that an investigative consumer report including information as to his character, general reputation, personal characteristics, and mode of living, whichever are applicable, may be made, and such disclosure (A) is made in a writing mailed, or otherwise delivered, to the consumer, not later than three days after the date on which the report was first requested, and (B) includes a statement informing the consumer of his right to request the additional disclosures provided for under subsection (b) of this section;

"(2) the report is to be used for employment purposes for which the consumer has not specifically applied.

"(b) Any person who procures or causes to be prepared

an investigative consumer report on any consumer shall, upon written request made by the consume within a reasonable period of time after receipt by his of the disclosure required by subsection (a) (1), shall make a complete and accurate disclosure of the nature and scope of the investigation requested. This disclosure shall be made in a writing mailed, or otherwise delivered, to the consumer not later that five days after the date on which the request for such disclosure was received from the consumer or such report was first requested, whichever is the later.

"(c) No person may be held liable for any violation of subsection (a) or (b) of this section if he shows by a preponderance of the evidence that at the time of the violation he maintained reasonable procedures to assure compliance with subsection (a) or (b).

"§607. Compliance procedures

"(a) Every consumer reporting agency shall maintain reasonable procedures designed to avoid violations of section 605 and to limit the furnishing of consumer reports to the purposes listed under section 604. These procedures shall require that prospective users of the information identify themselves, certify the purposes for which the information is sought, and certify that the information will be used for no other purpose. Every consumer reporting agency shall make a reasonable effort to verify the identity of a new prospective user and the uses certified by such prospective user prior to furnishing such user a consumer report. No consumer reporting agency may furnish a consumer report to any person if it has reasonable grounds for believing that the consumer report will not be used for a purpose listed in section 604.

"(b) Whenever a consumer reporting agency prepares a consumer report it shall follow reasonable procedures to assure maximum possible accuracy of the information concerning the individual about whom the report relates.

"§608. Disclosures to governmental agencies

"Notwithstanding the provisions of section 604, a consumer reporting agency may furnish identifying information respecting any consumer, limited to his name, address, former addresses, places of employment, o former places of employment, to a governmental agency.

"§609. Disclosures to consumers

"(a) Every consumer reporting agency shall, upon request and proper identification of any consumer, clearly and accurately disclose to the consumer:

"(1) The nature and substance of all information (except medical information) in its files on the consumer at the time of the request.

"(2) The sources of the information ; except that the sources of information acquired solely for use in preparing an investigative consumer report and actually used for no other purpose need not be disclosed: Provided, That in the event an action is brought under this title, such sources shall be available to the plaintiff under appropriate discovery procedures in the court in which the action is brought.

"(3) The recipients of any consumer report on the consumer which it has furnished—

"(A) for employment purposes within the two-year period preceding the request, and

"(B) for any other purpose within the six-month period

preceding the request.

"(b) The requirements of subsection (a) respecting the disclosure of sources of information and the recipients of consumer reports do not apply to information received or consumer reports furnished prior to the effective date of this title except to the extent that the matter involved is contained in the files of the consumer reporting agency on that date;

"§610 Conditions of disclosure to consumers

"(a) A consumer reporting agency shall make the disclosures required under section 609 during normal business hours and on reasonable notice.

"(b) The disclosures required under section 609 shall be made to the consumer—

"(1) in person if he appears in person and furnishes proper identification: or

"(2) by telephone if he has made a written request , with proper identification, for telephone disclosure and the toll charge, if any, for the telephone call is prepaid by or charged directly to the consumer.

"(c) Any consumer reporting agency shall provide trained personnel to explain to the consumer any information furnished to his pursuant to section 609.

"(d) The consumer shall be permitted to be accompanied by one other person of his choosing, who shall furnish reasonable identification. A consumer reporting agency may require the consumer to furnish a written statement granting permission to the consumer reporting agency to discuss the consumer's file in such person's presence.

"(e) Except as provided in sections 616 and 617, no

consumer may bring any action or proceeding in the nature of defamation, invasion of privacy, or negligence with respect to the reporting of information against any consumer reporting agency, any user of information, or any person who furnishes information to a consumer reporting agency, based on information disclosed pursuant to section 609, 610, or 615, except as to false information furnished with malice or willful intent to injure such consumer.

"§611. Procedure in case of disputed accuracy

"(a) If the completeness or accuracy of any item of information contained in his file is disputed by a consumer, and such dispute is directly conveyed to the consumer reporting agency by the consumer, the consumer reporting agency shall within a reasonable period of time reinvestigate and record the current status of that information unless it has reasonable grounds to believe that the dispute by the consumer is frivolous or irrelevant. If after such reinvestigation such information is found to be inaccurate or can no longer be verified, the consumer reporting agency shall promptly delete such information. The presence of contradictory information in the consumer's file does not in and of itself constitute reasonable grounds for believing the dispute is frivolous or irrelevant.

"(b) If the reinvestigation does not resolve the dispute, the consumer may file a brief statement setting forth the nature of the dispute. The consumer reporting agency may limit such statements to not more than one hundred words if it provides the consumer with assistance in writing a clear summary of the dispute.

"(c) Whenever a statement of a dispute is filed, unless

there is reasonable grounds to believe that it is frivolous or irrelevant, the consumer reporting agency shall, in any subsequent consumer report containing the information in question, clearly note that it is disputed by the consumer and provide either the consumer's statement or a clear and accurate codification or summary thereof.

"(d) Following any deletion of information which is found to be inaccurate or whose accuracy can no longer be verified or any notation as to disputed information, the consumer reporting agency shall, at the request of the consumer, furnish notification that the item has been deleted or the statement, codification or summary pursuant to subsection (b) or (c) to any person specifically designated by the consumer who has within two year prior thereto received a consumer report for employment purposes, or within six months prior thereto received a consumer report for any other purpose, which contained the deleted or disputed information. The consumer reporting agency shall clearly and conspicuously disclose to the consumer his rights to make such a request. Such disclosure shall be made at or prior to the time the information is deleted or the consumer's statement regarding the disputed information is received.

"**§612. Charges for certain disclosures**

"A consumer reporting agency shall make all disclosures pursuant to section 609 and furnish all consumer reports pursuant to section 611 (d) without charge to the consumer if, within thirty days after receipt by such consumer of a notification pursuant to section 615 or notification from a debt collection agency affiliated with such consumer reporting agency stating that the consumer's credit rating may be or has been adversely affected, the consumer makes a request under section 609 or 611 (d). Otherwise, the consumer reporting agency may impose a reasonable charge on the consumer for making disclosure to such consumer pursuant to section 609, the charge for which shall be indicated to the consumer prior to making disclosure; and for furnishing notifications, statements, summaries, or codifications to persons designated by the consumer pursuant to section 611 (d), the charge for which shall be indicated to the consumer prior to furnishing such information and shall not exceed the charge that the consumer reporting agency would impose on each designated recipient for a consumer report except that no charge may be made for notifying such persons of the deletion of information which is found to be inaccurate or which can no longer be verified.

"§613. Public record information for employment purposes

"A consumer reporting agency which furnishes a consumer report for employment purposes and which for that purpose complies and reports items of information on consumers which are matters of public record and are likely to have an adverse effect upon a consumer's ability to obtain employment shall—

"(1) at the time such public record information is reported to the user of such consumer report, notify the consumer of the fact that public record information is being reported by the consumer reporting agency, togeth er with the name and address of the person to whom such information is being reported; or

"(2) maintain strict procedures designed to insure that

whenever public record information which is likely to have an adverse effect on a consumer's ability to obtain employment is reported it is complete and up to date. For purposes of this paragraph, items of public record relating to arrests, indictments, convictions, suits, tax liens, and outstanding judgments shall be considered up to date if the current public record status of the item at the time of the report is reported.

"§614. Restrictions on investigative consumer reports.

"Whenever a consumer reporting agency prepares an investigative consumer report, no adverse information in the consumer report (other than information which is a matter of public record) may be included in a subsequent consumer report unless such adverse information has been verified in the process of making such subsequent consumer report, or the adverse information was received within the three-month period preceding the date the subsequent report is furnished.

"§615. Requirements on users of consumer reports

"(a) Whenever credit or insurance for personal, family, or household purposes, or employment involving a consumer is denied or the charge for such credit or insurance is increased either wholly or partly because of information contained in a consumer report from a consumer reporting agency, the user of the consumer report shall so advise the consumer against whom such adverse action has been taken and supply the name and address of the consumer reporting agency making the report.

"(b) Whenever credit for personal, family, or household purposes involving a consumer is denied or the charge for such credit is increased either wholly or partly because of information obtained from a person other than a consumer reporting agency bearing upon the consumer's credit worthiness, credit standing, credit capacity, character, general reputation, personal characteristics, or mode of living, the user of such information shall, within a reasonable period of time, upon the consumer's written request for the reasons for such adverse action received within sixty days after learning of such adverse action, disclose the nature of the information to the consumer. The user of such information shall clearly and accurately disclose to the consumer his right to make such written request at the time such adverse action is communicated to the consumer.

"(c) No person shall be held liable for any violation of the section if he shows by a preponderance of the evidence that at the time of the alleged violation he maintained reasonable procedures to assure compliance with the provisions of subsections (a) and (b).

"§616. Civil liability for willful noncompliance

"Any consumer reporting agency or use of information which willfully fails to comply with any requirement imposed under this title with respect to any consumer is liable to that consumer in an amount equal to the sum of—

"(1) any actual damages sustained by the consumer as a result of the failure;

"(2) such amount of punitive damages as the court may allow; and

"(3) in the case of any successful action to enforce any liability under this section, the costs of the action together with reasonable attorney's fees as determined by the court.

"§617. Civil liability for negligent noncompliance

"Any consumer reporting agency or user of information which is negligent in failing to comply with any requirement imposed under this title with respect to any consumer is liable to that consumer in an amount equal to the sum of —

"(1) any actual damages sustained by the consumer as a result of the failure;

"(2) in the case of any successful action to enforce any liability under this section, the costs of the action to enforce any liability under this section, the costs of the action together with reasonable attorney's fees as determined by the court.

"§618. Jurisdiction of courts; limitation of actions

"An action to enforce any liability created under this title may be brought in any appropriate United States district court without regard to the amount in controversy, or in any other court of competent jurisdiction, within two years form the date on which the liability arises, except that where a defendant has materially and willfully misrepresented any information required under this title to be disclosed to an individual and the information so misrepresented is material to the establishment of the defendant's liability to that individual under this title, the action may be brought at any time within two years after discovery by the individual of the misrepresentation.

"§619. Obtaining information under false pretenses

"Any officer or employee of a consumer reporting agency who knowingly and willfully provides information concerning an individual from the agency's files to a person not authorized to receive that information shall by fined not more that $5,000 or imprisoned not more than one year, or both.

"§621. Administrative enforcement

"(a) Compliance with the requirements imposed under this title shall be enforced under the Federal Trade Commission Act by the Federal Trade Commission with respect t to consumer reporting agencies and all other persons subject thereto, except to the extent that enforcement of the requirements imposed under this title is specifically committed to some other government agency under subsection (b) hereof. For the purpose of the exercise by the Federal Trade Commission of its functions and powers under the Federal Trade Commission Act, a violation of any requirement of prohibition imposed under this title shall constitute an unfair or deceptive act or practice in commerce in violation of section 5 (a) of the Federal Trade Commission Act and shall be subject to enforcement by the Federal Trade Commission pursuant to this subsection, irrespective of whether that person is engaged in commerce or meets any other jurisdictional tests in the Federal Trade Commission Act. The Federal Trade Commission shall have such procedural investigative, and enforcement powers, including the power to issue procedural rules in enforcing compliance with the requirements imposed under this title and to require the filing of reports, the production of documents, and the appearance of witnesses as though the applicable terms and conditions of the Federal Trade Commission Act were part of this title. Any person violating any of the provisions of this title shall be subject to the penalties and entitled to the privileges and immunities provided in the Federal Trade Commission Act as though the applicable terms and provisions thereof were part of this title.

"(b) Compliance with the requirements imposed under this title with respect to consumer reporting agencies and persons who use consumer reports from such agencies shall be enforced under—

"(1) section 8 of the Federal Deposit Insurance Act, in the case of:

"(A) national banks, by the Comptroller of the Currency;

"(B) member banks of the Federal Reserve System (other than national banks), by the Federal Reserve Board; and

"(C) banks insured by the Federal Deposit Insurance Corporation (other than members of the Federal Reserve System), by the Board of Directors of the Federal Deposit Insurance Corporation.'

"(2) section 5 (d) of the Home Owners Loan Act of 1933, section 407 of the National Housing Act, and sections 6 (i) and 17 of the Federal Home Loan Bank Act, by the Federal Home Loan Bank Board (acting directly or through the Federal Savings and Loan Insurance Corporation), in the case of any institution subject to any of those provisions;

"(3) the Federal Credit Union Act, by the Administrator of the National Credit Union Administration with respect to any Federal credit union;

"(4) the Acts to regulate commerce, by the Interstate Commerce Commission with respect to any common carrier subject go those Acts;

"(5) the Federal Aviation Act of 1958, by the Civil Aeronautics Board with respect to any air carrier or foreign air carrier subject to that Act; and

"(6) the Packers and Stockyards Act, 1921 (except as provided in section 406 of that Act), by the Secretary of Agriculture with respect to any activities subject to that Act.

"(c) For the purpose of the exercise by any agency referred to in subsection (b) of its powers under any Act referred to in that subsection, a violation of any requirement imposed under this title shall be deemed to be a violation of a requirement imposed under that Act. In addition to its powers under any provision of law specifically referred to in subsection (b), each of the agencies referred to in that subsection may exercise, for the purpose of enforcing compliance with any requirement imposed under this title any other authority conferred on it by law.

"§622. Relation to State laws

"This title does not annul, alter affect, or exempt any person subject to the provisions of this title from complying with the laws of any State with respect to the collection, distribution, or use of any information on consumers, except to the extent that those laws are inconsistent with any provision of this title, and then only to the extent of the inconsistency."

EFFECTIVE DATE

Sec. 602, Section 504 of the Consumer Credit Protection Act is amended by adding at the end thereof the following new subsection;

"(d) Title VI takes effect upon the expiration of one hundred and eighty days following the date of its enactment."

Approved October 26,1970

LEGISLATIVE HISTORY:

HOUSE REPORTS: No. 91-975 (Comm. on Banking and currency) and
No. 91-1587 (Comm. of Conference).
SENATE REPORT: No. 91-1139 accompanying S. 3678 (Comm. on Banking and Currency).
CONGRESSIONAL RECORD, Vol. 116 (1970):
May 25, considered and passed House.
Sept. 18, considered and passed Senate, amended.
Oct. 9, Senate agreed to conference report.
Oct. 13, House agreed to conference report.

Appendix X

FACTS FOR CONSUMERS FROM THE FTC

FAIR CREDIT REPORTING

- The Fair Credit Reporting Act protects you by requiring credit bureaus to furnish correct and complete information to businesses to use in evaluating your applications for credit, insurance, or a job.
- You have the right to know what information is in your credit report.
- Credit bureaus are required to conduct an investigation if you claim their information on you is inaccurate of incomplete.
- Legitimate adverse credit information generally stays on your credit report for seven years; information on bankruptcies can be reported for 10 years.
- Credit report can only be given to those persons, other than yourself, who have a legitimate business need for the information.

If you've ever applied for a charge account, a personal loan, insurance or a job, someone is probably keeping a file on you. This file might contain information on how you pay your bills, or whether you've been sued, arrested, or have filed for bankruptcy.

The companies that gather and sell this information are called "Credit Reporting Agencies," or "CRA's." The most common type of CRA is the credit bureau. The information sold by CRA's top creditors, employers, insurers, and other businesses is called a "consumer report." This report generally contains information about where you work and live and your bill-paying habits.

In 1970, Congress passed the Fair Credit Reporting Act to give consumers specific rights in dealing with CRA's. The Act protects you by requiring credit bureaus to furnish correct and complete information to businesses to use in evaluating your applications for credit, insurance, or a job.

The Federal Trade Commission enforces the Fair Credit Reporting Act. Here are answers to some questions about consumer reports and CRA's.

HOW DO I LOCATE THE CRA THAT HAS MY FILE?

If your application was denied because of information supplied by a CRA, that agency's name and address must be supplied to you by the company you applied to. Otherwise, you can find the CRA that has your file by calling those listed in the Yellow Pages under "credit" or "credit rating and reporting." Since more than one CRA may have a file about you, call each one listed until you locate all agencies maintaining your file.

DO I HAVE THE RIGHT TO KNOW
WHAT THE REPORT SAYS?

Yes, if you request it. The CRA is required to tell you about every piece of information in the report, and in most cases, the sources of that information. Medical information is exempt from this rule, but you can have your physician try to obtain it for you. The CRA is not required to give you a copy of the report, although more and more are doing so. You also have the right to be told the name of anyone who received a report on you in the past six months.(If your inquiry concerns a job application, you can get the names of those who received a report during the past two years.)

IN THIS INFORMATION FREE?

Yes, if your application was denied because of information furnished by the CRA, and if you request it within 30 days of receiving the denial notice. If you don't meet these requirements, the CRA may charge a reasonable fee.

WHAT CAN I DO IF THE INFORMATION IS INACCURATE OR INCOMPLETE?

Notify the CRA. They're required to reinvestigate the items in question. If the new investigation reveals an error, a corrected version will be sent, on your request, to anyone who received your report in the past sic months. (Job applicants can have corrected reports sent to anyone who received a copy during the past two years.)

WHAT CAN I DO IF THE CRA WON'T MODIFY MY REPORT?

The new investigation may not resolve your dispute with the CRA. If this happens, have the CRA include your version or a summary of your version of the disputed information in your file an in future reports. At your request, the CRA also will show your version to anyone who recently received a copy of the old report. There is no charge for this service if it's requested within 30 days after y you receive notice of your application denial. After that, there may be a reasonable charge.

DO I HAVE TO GO IN PERSON TO GET THE INFORMATION?

No, you also may request information over the phone. But before the CRA will provide information, you must establish your identity by completing forms they will send you. If you do wish to visit in person, you'll need to make an appointment.

ARE REPORTS PREPARED ON INSURANCE AND JOB APPLICANTS DIFFERENT?

If a report is prepared on you in response to an insurance or job application, it may be an investigative consumer report. These are much more detailed that regular consumer reports. They often involve interviews with acquaintances about your lifestyle, character, and reputation. Unlike regular consumer reports, you'll be notified in writing when a company orders an investigate report about you. This notice also will explain your right to ask for additional information about the report from the company you applied to. If your application is rejected however, you may prefer to obtain a complete disclosure by contacting the CRA, as outlined in this brochure. Note that the CRA does not have to reveal the sources of the investigative information.

How long can CRA's report unfavorable information?

Generally, seven years. Adverse information can't be reported after that, with certain exceptions:
- bankruptcy information can be reported for 10 years;
- information reported because of an application for a job with a salary of more that $20,000 has no time

limitation;

- information concerning a lawsuit or a judgment against you can be reported for seven years or until the statute of limitations runs out, whichever is longer.

CAN ANYONE GET A COPY OF THE REPORT?

No, it's only given to those with a legitimate business need.

ARE THERE OTHER LAWS I SHOULD KNOW ABOUT?

Yes, is you applied for and were denied credit, the Equal Credit Opportunity Act requires creditors to tell you the specific reasons for y our denial. For example, the creditor must tell you whether the denial was because you have "no credit file" with a CRA or because the CRA says you have "delinquent obligations." This law also requires creditors to consider, upon request, additional information you might supply about your credit history.

You may wish to obtain the reason for the denial from the creditor before you go to the credit bureau.

DO WOMEN HAVE SPECIAL PROBLEMS WITH CREDIT APPLICATIONS?

Married and formerly married women may encounter some common credit-related problems. For more information, write for the free FTC brochure, Women and Credit Histories, Public Reference, Federal Trade Commission, Washington, D. C. 20580.

WHERE SHOULD I REPORT VIOLATIONS OF THE LAW?

Although the FTC can't act as your lawyer in private disputes, information about your experiences and concerns is vital to the enforcement of the Fair Credit Reporting Act. Please send questions or complaints to: Correspondence Branch, Federal Trade Commission, Washington, D. C. 20580.

FAIR CREDIT BILLING

- The Fair credit Billing Act generally applies to "open end" credit accounts that include: credit cards, revolving charge accounts, and overdraft checking.
- If you find a mistake on your bill, you must send a separate written billing error notice to the creditor. It must reach the creditor within 60 days after the first bill containing the error was mailed to you.
- Your billing error notice must be acknowledged by the creditor in writing within 30 days after it is received, unless the problem is resolved within that period.
- While a bill is being disputed, the creditor may not threaten to damage your credit rating or report you as delinquent to anyone.

Has the department store's computer ever billed you for merchandise you returned to the store or never received? Or has the credit card company ever charged you twice for the same item or failed to properly credit a payment made on your account? Credit billing errors do occur, but they are easy to resolve if you know how to use the Fair Credit Billing Act (FCBA). Congress passed this law in 1975 to help consumers resolve disputes with creditors and to ensure fair handling of credit accounts.

WHICH CREDIT TRANSACTIONS ARE COVERED?

The FCBA generally applies only to "open end" credit accounts. Open end accounts include credit cards, revolving charge accounts (such as department store accounts), and overdraft checking. The periodic bills, or billing statements, you receive (usually monthly) for such accounts are covered by the FCBA. The Act does not apply to loan or credit sales which are paid according to a fixed schedule until the entire amount is paid back.

WHAT TYPES OF DISPUTES ARE COVERED?

The FCBA settlement procedure applies only to disputes over "billing errors" on periodic statements, such as the following:

- Charges not made by you or anyone authorized to use your account.
- Charges which are incorrectly identified or for which the wrong amount or date is shown.
- Charges for goods and services you did not accept or which were not delivered as agreed.
- Computational or similar errors.
- Failure to properly reflect payments or other credits, such as returns.
- Not mailing or delivering bills to your current address (provided you give a change of address at least 20 days before the billing period ends).
- Charges of which you request an explanation or written proof of purchase.

HOW TO USE THE SETTLEMENT PROCEDURE

When many consumers find a mistake on their bill, they pick up the phone and call the company to correct the problem. You can do this if you wish, but phoning does not trigger the legal safeguards under the FCBA.

To be protected under the law, you must send a separate written billing error notice to the creditor. Your notice must reach the creditor within 60 days after the first bill containing the error was mailed to you. Send the notice to the address provided on the bill for billing error notices (and not, or example, directly to the store, unless the bill says that's where it should be sent). In your letter, you must include the following information:

- Your name and account number.
- A statement that you believe the bill contains a billing error and the dollar amount involved.
- The reasons why you believe there is a mistake.

It's a good idea to send it by certified mail, with a return receipt requested. That way you'll have proof of the dates of mailing and receipt. If you wish, send photocopies of sales slips or other documents, but keep the originals for your records.

WHAT MUST THE CREDITOR DO?

Your letter claiming a billing error must be acknowledged by the creditor in writing *within 30 days* after it is received, unless the problem is resolved within that period. In any case, within two billing cycles (but not more than 90 days), the creditor *must* conduct a reasonable investigation and either correct the mistake or explain why the bill is believed to be correct.

WHAT HAPPENS WHILE A BILL IS BEING DISPUTED?

You may withhold payment of the amount in dispute including the affected portions of minimum payments and finance charges until the dispute is resolved. You are still required to pay any part of the bill which is not disputed, including finance and other charges on undisputed amounts.

While the FCBA dispute settlement procedure is going on, the creditor may not take any legal or other action to collect the amount in dispute. Your account may not be closed or restricted in any way, except that the disputed amount may be applied against your credit limit.

WHAT ABOUT YOUR CREDIT RATING?

While a bill is being disputed, the creditor may not threaten to damage y our credit rating or report you as delinquent to anyone. however, the creditor is permitted to report that you are disputing your bill.

Another federal law, the Equal Credit Opportunity Act, prohibits creditors from discriminating against credit applicants who, in good faith, exercise their rights under the FCBA. You cannot be denied credit merely because you have disputed a bill.

IF THE CREDITOR MAKES A MISTAKE

If your bill is found to contain a billing error, the creditor must write you explaining the corrections to be made on your account. In addition to crediting your account with the amount not owed, the creditor must remove all finance charges, late fees, or other charges relating to that amount. If the creditor concludes that you owe part of the disputed amount, this must be explained in writing. You also have the right to request copies of documents proving you owe the money.

IF THE BILL IS CORRECT

If the creditor investigates and still believes the bill is correct, you must be told promptly in writing how much you owe and why. You may also ask for copies of relevant docu-ments. At this point, you will owe the disputed amount, plus any finance charges that accumulated while it was dis-puted. You may also have to pay the minimum payment amount missed because of the dispute.

IF YOU STILL DISAGREE

Even after the FCBA dispute settlement procedure has ended, you may still feel the bill is wrong. If this happens, write the creditor within 10 days after receiving the explanation and say you still refuse to pay the disputed amount. At this point, the creditor may begin collection procedures. However, if the creditor reports you to a credit bureau as delinquent, he must also state that you don't think you owe the money. Also, you must be told who receives such reports.

IF THE CREDITOR DOESN'T FOLLOW THE PROCEDURES

Any creditor who fails to follow the FCBA dispute settlement procedure may not collect the amount in dispute, or any finance charges on it, up to $50, *even if the bill turns out to be correct*. For example, this penalty would apply if a creditor acknowledges your complaint in 45 days (15 days too late) or takes more than two billing cycles to resolve a dispute. It also applies if a creditor threatens to report—or goes ahead and improperly reports—your nonpayments to anyone. You also have the right, as more fully described below, to sue a creditor for any violation of the FCBA.

COMPLAINTS ABOUT QUALITY

Disputes about the *quality* of goods and services are not necessarily "billing errors," so the dispute procedure may not apply. However, if you purchase unsatisfactory goods or services with a credit card, the FCBA allows you to take the same legal actions against the credit card issuer as you could take under state law against the seller. If your state law permits you to withhold payment to a seller for defective merchandise, or pay and sue for a refund, you might also be able to withhold payment to the credit card issuer. Because state laws on your right to stop payment vary, it is best to get legal advice before you do so.

However, before you take legal action, you must give the seller a chance to remedy the problem. Also, unless the seller is also the card issuer (such as a company that issued you a gasoline credit card), you must have bought the item in your home state or within 100 miles of your current mailing address, and the amount charged must have been more than $50.

OTHER BILLING RIGHTS FOR CONSUMERS

The FCBA also requires "open-end" creditors to do the following for their customers:
- Give you a written notice when you open a new account, and at other specified times, describing your right to dispute billing errors.
- Provide a statement for each billing period in which you owe—or they owe you—more than $1.00.
- Mail or deliver your bill to you at least 14 days before the payment is due, if you are given a time period

within which to pay the bill without incurring additional finance or other charges.

- Credit all payments to your accounts as of the date they are received, unless not doing so would not result in extra charges.
- Promptly credit or refund overpayments.

YOU CAN ALSO SUE

You can sue a creditor who violates any FCBA provisions. If you win, you may be awarded damages resulting from the violation, plus twice the amount of any finance charge (not less than $100 or more than $1,000.) The court may also order the creditor to pay your attorney's fees and costs. If possible, retain a private attorney who is willing to accept whatever the fee the court awards as the entire fee for representing you. Some lawyers may not be willing to accept your case unless you agree to pay their fee—win or lose—or if you will add to a fee awarded by the court but which they believe is too low. Be sure you get a full explanation of what it could cost before you go to court.

WHERE TO REPORT FCBA VIOLATIONS

The Federal Trade Commission (FTC) enforces the FCBA for almost all creditors except banks. While the Commission does represent individuals in private disputes, information from consumers as to their experiences and concerns is vital to the enforcement of the Act. Questions or complaints may be addressed to the nearest FTC Regional Office. If they concern national creditors, write: Correspondence Branch, Federal Trade Commission, Washington, D.C. 20580.

FAIR DEBT COLLECTION

- If you fall behind in paying your creditors, or an error is made on your accounts, you may be contacted by a "debt collector."
- Collectors may not harass, oppress, or abuse you.
- Collectors may not use any false statements when collecting a debt.
- Debt collectors may not engage in unfair practices in attempting to collect a debt.
- You have the right to sue a collector in a state or federal court within one year from the date you believe the law was violated.

If you use credit cards, owe money on a personal loan, or are paying on a home mortgage, you are a "debtor." If you fall behind in repaying your creditors, or an error is made on your accounts, you maybe contacted by a "debt collector."

You should know that in either situation the Fair Debt Collection Practices Act requires that debt collectors treat you fairly by prohibiting certain methods of debt collection. Of course, the law does no forgive any legitimate debt you owe.

This brochure provides answers to commonly asked questions to help you understand your rights under the Fair Debt Collection Practices Act.

WHAT DEBTS ARE COVERED?

Personal, family, and household debts are covered under the Act. This includes money owed for the purchase of an automobile, for medical care, or for charge accounts.

FACTS FOR CONSUMERS FROM THE FTC

WHO IS A DEBT COLLECTOR?

A debt collector is any person, other than the creditor, who regularly collects debts owed to others. Under a 1986 amendment to the Fair Debt Collection Practices Act, this includes attorneys who collect debts on a regular basis.

HOW MAY A DEBT COLLECTOR CONTACT YOU?

A collector may contact you in person, by mail, telephone, telegram, or FAX. However, a debt collector may not contact you at unreasonable times or places, such as before 8 a.m. or after 9 p.m., unless you agree. A debt collector also may not contact you at work if the collector knows that your employer disapproves.

CAN YOU STOP A DEBT COLLECTOR FROM CONTACTING YOU?

You may stop a collector from contacting you by writing a letter to the collection agency telling them to stop. Once the agency receives your letter, they may not contact you again except to say there will be no further contact. Another exception is that the agency may notify you if the debt collector or the creditor intends to take some specific action.

MAY A DEBT COLLECTOR CONTACT ANY PERSON OTHER THAN YOU CONCERNING YOUR DEBT?

If you have am attorney, the debt collector may not contact anyone other than your attorney. If you do not have an attorney, a collector may contact other people, but only to find out where you live and work. Collectors usually are prohibited from contacting such permissible third parties

199

more than once. In most cases, the collector is not permitted to tell anyone other than you and your attorney that you owe money.

WHAT IS THE DEBT COLLECTOR REQUIRED TO TELL YOU ABOUT THE DEBT?

Within five days after you are first contacted, the collector must send you a written notice telling you the amount of money you owe; the name of the creditor to whom you owe the money; and what action to take if you believe you do not owe the money.

MAY A DEBT COLLECTOR CONTINUE TO CONTACT YOU IF YOU BELIEVE YOU DO NOT OWE MONEY?

A collector may not contact you if, within 30 days after you are first contacted, you send the collection agency a letter stating you do not owe money. However, a collector can renew collection activities if you are sent proof of the debt, such as a copy of a bill for the amount owed.

WHAT TYPES OF DEBT COLLECTION PRACTICES ARE PROHIBITED?

Harassment. Debt collectors may not harass, oppress, o abuse any person. For example, debt collectors may not:
- use threats of violence or harm against the person, property, or reputation;
- publish a lit of consumers who refuse to pay their debts (except to a credit bureau);
- use obscene or profane language;
- repeatedly use the telephone to annoy someone;

- telephone people without identifying themselves;
- advertise your debt.

False statements. Debt collectors may not use any false statements when collecting a debt. For example, debt collectors may not:
- falsely imply that they are attorneys or government representatives;
- falsely imply that you have committed a crime;
- falsely represent that they operate or work for a credit bureau;
- misrepresent the amount of your debt;
- misrepresent the involvement of an attorney in collecting a debt;
- indicate that papers being sent to you are legal forms when they are not;
- indicate that papers being sent to you are not legal forms when they are.

Debt collectors also may not state that:
- you will be arrested if you do not pay your debt.
- they will seize, garnish, attach, or sell your property or wages, unless the collection agency or creditor intends to do so, and it is legal to do so;
- actions, such as a lawsuit, will be taken against you, which legally may not be taken, or which they do not intend to take.

Debt collectors may not:
- give false credit information about you to anyone;

- send you anything that looks like an official document from a court or government agency when it is not;
- use a false name.

Unfair practices. Debt collectors may not engage in unfair practices in attempting to collect a debt. For example, collectors may not;
- collect any amount greater than your debt, unless allowed by law;
- deposit a post-dated check prematurely;
- make you accept collect calls or pay for telegrams;
- take or threaten to take your property unless this can be cone legally;
- contact you by postcard.

WHAT CONTROL DO YOU HAVE OVER PAYMENT OF DEBTS?

If you owe more than one debt, any payment you make must be applied to the debt you indicate. A debt collector may not apply a payment to any debt you believe you do not owe.

WHAT CAN YOU DO IF YOU BELIEVE A DEBT COLLECTOR VIOLATED THE LAW?

You have the right to sue a collector in a state of federal court within one year from the date you believe the law was violated. If you win, you may recover money for the damages you suffered. Court costs and attorney's fees also can be recovered. A group of people also may sue a debt collector and recover money for damages up to $5000,000, or one percent of the collector's net worth, whichever is less.

WHERE CAN YOU REPORT A DEBT COLLECTOR FOR AN ALLEGED VIOLATION OF THE LAW?

Report any problems you have with a debt collector to your state Attorney General's office and the Federal Trade Commission. Many states also have their own debt collection laws and your Attorney General's office can help you determine your rights.

If you have questions about the Fair Debt Collection Practices Act, or your rights under the Act, write: Correspondence Branch, Federal Trade Commission, Washington, D. C. 20580. Although the FTC generally cannot intervene in individual disputes, the information you provide may indicate a pattern of possible law violations requiring action by the Commission.

EQUAL CREDIT OPPORTUNITY

When applying for credit, a creditor **may not**, among other things:

- Discourage you from applying because of your sex, marital status, age, national origin, or because you receive public assistance income.
- Ask whether you are divorced or widowed.
- Ask about your plans for having or raising children.
- Refuse to consider reliable public assistance income in the same manner as other income.
- Consider the race of the people in your neighborhood where you want to buy or improve a house with borrowed money.
- Refuse to consider consistently received alimony, child support, or separate maintenance payments.

If you still think only of credit cards when you hear the word "credit," think again. Credit is used by millions of consumers for a variety of purposes: to finance educations, remodel homes, obtain small business loans, and for home mortgages.

A law passed by Congress ensures that all consumers will be given an equal chance to receive credit. The Equal Credit Opportunity Act says it is illegal for creditors to discriminate against applicants on the basis of their sex, marital status, race, national origin, religion, age or because they get public assistance income. This does not mean all consumers who apply for credit will get it. Creditors can still use factors such as income, expense, debts, and credit history to judge applicants.

The law protects you when dealing with any creditor who regularly extends credit, including: banks, small loan and finance companies, retail and department stores, credit card companies, and credit unions. Anyone participating in the decision to grant credit, such as real estate brokers who arrange financing, is covered by the law. Businesses applying for credit are protected by the law, too.

Consumers have equal rights in every phase of the credit application process. Here is a checklist of important rights to remember when you request credit:

WHEN YOU APPLY FOR CREDIT, A CREDITOR MAY NOT...

- Discourage you from applying because of your sex, marital status, age, national origin, or because you receive public assistance income.
- Ask you to reveal your sex, race, national origin, or religion. A creditor may ask you to voluntarily disclose this information if you are applying for a real estate loan. This information helps federal agencies enforce anti-discrimination laws. A creditor may ask what your residence of immigration status is.
- Ask whether you are divorced or widowed.
- Ask what your marital status is if you are applying for a separate, unsecured account. A creditor may ask you to reveal this information of you live in the "community property" states: Arizona, California, Idaho, Louisiana, Nevada, New Mexico, Texas, and Washington. In any state, a creditor may ask for this information if you apply for a joint account or any account secured by property.

- Ask you for information about your husband or wife. A creditor may ask about your spouse if: your spouse is applying with you; your spouse will be allowed to use the account; you are relying on your spouse's income or on alimony or child support income from a former spouse; or if you reside in a community property state (listed above).
- Ask about your plans for having or raisin children.
- Ask if you receive alimony, child support, or separate maintenance payments. A creditor may ask for this information if you are first told that you don't have to reveal it if you won't rely on it to get credit. A creditor may ask if you have to pay alimony, child support, or separate maintenance payments.

WHEN DECIDING TO GIVE YOU CREDIT, A CREDITOR MAY NOT. . .

- Consider you sex, marital status, race, national origin, or religion.
- Consider whether you have a telephone listing in your name. A creditor may consider whether there is a shone in your home.
- Consider the race of the people who live in the neighborhood where you want to buy or improve a house with borrowed money.
- Consider your age, with certain exceptions:
  —if you are too young to sign contracts. Generally, this applies to those 18 and under.
  —if you are 62 or over, and the creditor will favor you because of your age.
  —if it is used to determine the meaning of other factors

which are important to credit-worthiness. For example, a creditor could use your age to see if your income might be reduced because you are about to retire.

—if it is used in a scoring system which factors applicants age 62 and over. A credit-scoring system assigns different points to your answers to application questions. For example, owning a home might be worth 5. The total number of points helps the creditor to decide if you are credit-worthy.

WHEN EVALUATING YOUR INCOME, A CREDITOR MAY NOT . . .

- Refuse to consider reliable public assistance income in same manner as other income.
- Discount income because of your sex or marital status. For example, a creditor cannot count a man's salary at 100% and a woman's at 75%. A creditor may not assume a woman of child-bearing age will stop work to raise children.
- Discount or refuse to consider income because it is derived from part-time employment or from pension, annuity, or retirement benefits programs.
- Refuse to consider consistently-received alimony, child support, or separate maintenance payments. A creditor may ask you for proof that this income has been received consistently.

YOU ALSO HAVE THE RIGHT . . .

- To have credit in your birth name (Mary Smith), your first and your spouse's last name (Mary Jones), or your first name and a combined last name (Mary Smith-Jones).

- To get credit without a co-signer, if you meet the creditor's standards.
- To have a co-signer other than your husband or wife, if one is necessary.
- To keep your own accounts after you change your name, marital status, reach a certain age, or retire, unless the creditor had evidence that you are unable or unwilling to pay.
- To know whether your application was accepted or rejected within 30 days of filing it.
- To knowing why your application was rejected. The creditor must either immediately give you the specific reasons for your rejection or tell you of your right to learn the reason if you ask them within 60 days. (Examples of reasons are:"your income was low," or "You haven't been employed long enough." Examples of unacceptable reasons are: "You didn't meet our minimum standards," or "You didn't receive enough points on our credit-scoring system.") Indefinite and vague reasons are illegal—ask for specifics.
- To learn the specific reasons why you were offered less favorable terms than you applied for. Example of less favorable terms include higher finance charges or less money than you requested. This does not hold if you accept the less favorable terms.
- To know the specific reasons why your account was closed or why the terms of the account were made less favorable to you. This does not hold if these actions

were taken because your account was delinquent or because you have not used the account for some time.

A SPECIAL NOTE TO WOMEN

A good credit history, a record of how you paid past bills, is often necessary to obtain credit. Unfortunately, this hurts many married, separated, divorced, and widowed women. There are two common reasons women do not have credit histories in their own names: they lost their credit histories when they married and changed their names: or creditors reported accounts shared by married couples in the husband's name only.

The law says when creditors report histories to credit bureaus or to other creditors they must report information on accounts shared by married couples in both names. This is true only for accounts opened after June 1, 1977. Also, if you and your spouse opened an account before that time, you should ask the creditor to use both names.

If you are married, divorced, separated, or widowed, you should make a special point to call or visit your local credit bureau(s) to ensure that all relevant information is in a file under your own name. To learn more about building your credit file, send for the free brochure, *Women and Credit Histories*, by writing: Public Reference, Federal Trade Commission, Washington, D.C. 20580.

WHAT YOU CAN DO IF YOU SUSPECT DISCRIMINATION...

- Complain to the creditor. Make it known that you are aware of the law. The creditor may reverse the decision or detect an error.

- Many states have their own equal credit opportunity laws. Check with your state's Attorney General's office to see if the creditor violated state laws. Your state may decide to take the creditor to court.
- Bring a case in Federal district court. If you win, you can recover your damages and be awarded a penalty. You can also recover reasonable attorney's' fees and court costs. An attorney can advise you on how to proceed.
- Join with others to file a class action suit. You may recover punitive damages for the class of up to $5000,000 or 1% of the creditor's net worth, whichever is less.
- Report violations to the appropriate government agency. If you are denied credit, the creditor must give you the name and address of the agency to contact. While the agencies do not resolve individual complaints, they do use consumer comments to decide which companies to investigate. A list of agencies appear at the end of this chapter.

WHERE TO SEND COMPLAINTS AND QUESTIONS

If a retail store, department store, small loan and finance company, mortgage company, oil company, public utility company, state credit union, government lending program, or travel and expense credit card company is involved, contact the Federal Trade Commission office nearest y you:

If your complaint concerns a nationally-chartered make (National or N.A. will be part of the name), write to:

Comptroller of the Currency
Compliance Management
Mail Stop 7-5
Washington, D. C. 20219

If your complaint concerns a state-chartered bank that is insured by the Federal Deposit Insurance Corporation but is not a member of the Federal Reserve System, write to:
Federal Deposit Insurance Corporation
Consumer Affairs Division
Washington, D. C. 20429

If your complaint concerns a federally-chartered or federally-insured savings and loan association, write to:
Office of Thrift Supervision
Consumer Affairs Program
Washington, D. C. 20552

If your complaint concerns a federally-chartered credit union, write to:
National Credit Union Administration
Consumer Affairs Division
Washington, D. C. 20456

Complaints against all kinds of creditors can be referred to:
Department of Justice
Civil Rights Division
Washington, D. C. 20530

Appendix Y

THE FAIR DEBT COLLECTION PRACTICES ACT

Public law #95-109

AN ACT

To amend the Consumer Credit Protection Act to prohibit abusive practices by debt collectors.

Be it enacted by the Senate and House of Representatives of the United States of America in Congress assembled, That the Consumer Credit Protection Act (15 U.S.C. 1601 et seq.) is amended by adding at the end thereof the following new title:

TITLE VIII—DEBT COLLECTION PRACTICES

"Sec.
"801. Short title.
"802. Findings and purpose.
"803. Definitions.
"804. Acquisition of location information.
"805. Communication in connection with debt collection.
"806. Harassment or abuse.
"807. False or misleading representations.

"808. Unfair practices.

"809. Validation of debts.

"810. Multiple debts.

"811. Legal actions by debt collectors.

"812. Furnishing certain deceptive forms.

"813. Civil liability.

"814. Administrative enforcement.

"815. Reports to Congress by the Commission.

"816. Relation to State laws.

"817. Exemption for State regulation.

"818. Effective date.

"§801. Short title

"This title may be cited as the 'Fair Debt Collection Practices Act'.

"§802. Findings and purpose

"(a) There is abundant evidence of the use of abusive, deceptive, and unfair debt collection practices by many debt collectors. Abusive debt collection practices contribute to the number of personal bankruptcies., to marital instability, to the loss of jobs, and to invasions of individual privacy.

"(b) Existing laws and procedures for redressing these injuries are inadequate to protect consumers.

"(c) Means other than misrepresentation or other abusive debt collection practices are available for the effective collection of debts.

"(d) Abusive debt collection practices are carried on to a substantial extent in interstate commerce and through means and instrumentalities of such commerce. Even where abusive debt collection practices are purely intrastate in character, they nevertheless directly affect interstate commerce."(e) It is the purpose of this title to eliminate abusive debt collection practices by debt collectors, to issuer that those debt collection practices are not competitively disadvantaged, and to promote consistent State action to protect consumers against debt collection abuses.

"§803. Definitions

"As used in this title—

"(1) The term "Commission" means the Federal Trade Commission.

"(2) The term "communication" means the conveying of information regarding a debt directly or indirectly to any person through any medium.

"(3) The term "consumer" means any natural person obligated or allegedly obligated to pay any debt.

"(4) The term "Creditor"means any person who offers or extends credit creating a debt or to whom a debt is owed, but such term does not include any person to the extent that he receives an assignment or transfer of a debt in default solely for the purpose of facilitating collection of such debt for another.

"(5) The term "debt" means any obligation or alleged obligation of a consumer to pay money arising out of a transaction in which the money, property, insurance, or services which are the subject of the transaction are primarily for personal, family;y, or household purposes, whether or not such obligation has been reduced to judgment.

"(6) The term "debt collector" means any person who uses any instrumentality of interstate commerce of the mails in any business the principal purpose of which is the collection of any debts, or who regularly collects or attempts to collect, directly or indirectly, debts owed or due or asserted to be owed or due another. Notwithstanding the exclusion provided by clause (F) the t last sentence of this paragraph, the term includes any creditor who, in the process of collecting his own debts, uses any name other than his own which would indicate that a purpose of Section 808(6), such term also includes any person who uses any instrumentality of interstate commerce of the mails in any business the principal purpose of which is the enforcement of security interests. The term does not include

"(A) any officer or employee of a creditor while, in the name of the creditor, collecting debts for such creditor;

"(B) any person while acting as a debt collector for another person, both of whom are related by common ownership or affiliated by corporated control, if the person acting as a debt collector does so onlyfor persons to who it is so relateed or affiliated and if the principal business of such person is not the collection of debts;

"(C) any officer or employee of the United States or any State to the rextent that collecting o attempting to collect any debt is in the performance of his official duties;

"(D) any person while serving or attempting to serve legal process on any other person in connection with the judicial enforcement of any debt;

"(E) any nonprofit organization which, at the request of consumers, performs bona fide consumer credit counseling and assists consumers in the liquidation of their debts by receiving payments from such consumers and distributing such amounts to creditors; and

"(F) any person collecting or attempting to collect any debt owed or due or asserted to be owed or due another to the extent such activity (i) is incidental to a bona fide fiduciary obligation or a bona fide escrow arrangement; (ii) concerns a debt which was originated by such person; (iii) concerns a debt which was not in default at the time it was obtained by such person; or (iv) concerns a debt obtained by such person as a secured party in a commercial credit transaction involving the creditor.

"(7) The term "location information" means a consumer's place of abode and his telephone number at such place, or his place of employment.

"(8) The term "State" means any State, territory, or possession of the United States, the District of Columbia, the Commonwealth of Puerto Rico, or any political subdivision of any of the foregoing.

"§804. Acquisition of location information

"Any debt collector communicating with any person other than the consumer for the purpose of acquiring location information about the consumer shall—

"(1) identify himself, state that he is confirming or correcting location information concerning the consumer, and, only if expressly requested, identify his employer;

"(2) not state that such consumer owes any debt;

"(3) not communicate with any such person more

unless the debt collector reasonably believes that the earlier response of such person is erroneous or incomplete and that such person now has correct or complete location information:

(4) not communicate by post card;

(5) not use any language or symbol on any envelope or in the contents of any communication effected by the mails or telegram that indicates that the debt collector is in the debt collection business or that the communication related to the collection of a debt; and

(6) after the debt collector knows the consumer is represented by an attorney with regard to the subject debt and has knowledge of, or can readily ascertain, such attorney's name and address, not communicate with any person other than that attorney unless the attorney fails to respond within a reasonable period of time to communication from the debt collector.

"§ 805. Communication in connection with debt collection

"(a) Communication with the consumer generally. — Without the prior consent of the consumer given directly to the debt collector or the express permission of a court of competent jurisdiction, a debt collector may not communicate with a consumer in connection with the collection of any debt—

"(1) at any unusual time or place or a time or place known or which should be known to be inconvenient to the consumer. In the absence of knowledge of circumstances to the contrary, a debt collector shall assume that the convenient time for communicating

assume that the convenient time for communicating with a consumer is after 8 o'clock ante meridiem and before 9 o'clock post meridiem local time at the consumer's location;

"(2) if the debt collector knows the consumer is represented by an attorney with respect to such debt and has knowledge of, or can readily ascertain, such attorney's name and address, unless the attorney fails to respond within a reasonable period of time to a communication from the debt collector or unless the attorney consents to direct communication with the consumer; or

"(3) at the consumer's place of employment if the debt collector knows or has reason to know that the consumer's employer prohibits the consumer from receiving such communication.

"(b) Communication with third parties. — Except as provided in section 804, without the prior consent of the consumer given directly to the debt collector, or the express permission of a court of competent jurisdiction, or as reasonable necessary to effectuate a post judgment judicial remedy, a debt collector may not communicate, in connection with the collection of any debt, with any person other than the consumer, his attorney, a consumer reporting agency if otherwise permitted by law, the creditor, the attorney of the creditor, or the attorney of the debt collector.

"(c) Ceasing communication—If a consumer notifies a debt collector in writing that the consumer refuses to pay a debt or that the consumer wishes the debt collector to cease further communication with the consumer, the debt collector shall not communicate further with the consumer with respect to such debt, except—

"(1) to advise the consumer that the debt collector's further efforts are being terminated;

"(2) to notify the consumer that the debt collector or creditor may invoke specified remedies which are ordinarily invoked by such debt collector or creditor; or

"(3) where applicable, to notify the consumer that the debt collector or creditor intends to invoke a specified remedy.

If such notice from the consumer is made by mail, notification shall be complete upon receipt.

"(d) For the purpose of this section, the term "consumer" includes the consumer's spouse, parent (if the consumer is a minor), guardian, executor, or administrator.

"§806. Harassment or abuse

"A debt collector may not engage in any conduct the natural consequence of which is to harass, oppress, or abuse any person in connection with the collection of a debt. Without limiting the general application of the foregoing, the following conduct is a violation of this section:

"(1) The use or threat of use of violence or other criminal means to harm the physical person, reputation, or property of any person.

"(2) The use of obscene or profane language or language the natural consequence of which is to abuse the hearer or reader.

"(3) The publication of a list of consumers who allegedly refuse to pay debts, except to a consumer reporting agency or the persons meeting the requirements of section 603(f) or 604(3) of this Act.

"(4) The advertisement for sale of any debt to coerce payment of the debt.

"(5) Causing a telephone to ring or engaging any person in telephone conversation repeatedly or continuously with intent to annoy, abuse, or harass any person at the called number.

"(6) Except as provided in section 804, the placement of telephone calls without meaningful disclosure of the caller's identity.

"§807. False or misleading representations

"A debt collector may not use any false, deceptive, or misleading representation or means in connection with the collection of any debt. Without limiting the general application of the foregoing, the following conduct is a violation of this section:

"(1) The false representation or implication that the debt collector is vouched for, bonded by, or affiliated with the United States or any State, including the use of any badge, uniform or facsimile thereof.

"(2) The false representation of —

"(A) the character, amount, or legal status of any debt; or

"(B) any services rendered or compensation which may be lawfully receiveby any debt collector for the collection of a debt.

"(3) The false representation or implication that any individual is an attorney or that any communication is from an attorney.

"(4) The representation or implication that nonpayment of any debt will result in the arrest or imprisonment of any person or the seizure, garnishment, attachment, or sale of any property or wages of any person unless such action is lawful and the debt collector or creditor intends to take such action.

"(5) The threat to take any action that cannot legally be taken or that is not intended to be taken.

"(6) The false representation or implication that a sale, referral, or other transfer of any interest in a debt shall cause the consumer to—

"(A) lose any claim or defense to payment of the debt; or

"(B) become subject to any practice prohibited by this title.

"(7) The false representation of implication that the consumer committed any crime or other conduct in order to disgrace the consumer.

"(8) Communicating or threatening to communicate to any person credit information which is known or which should be known to be false, including the failure to communicate that a disputed debt is disputed.

"(9) The use or distribution of any written communication which simulates or is falsely represented to be a document authorized, issued, or approved by any court, official, or agency of the United States or any State, or which creates a false impression as to its source, authorization, or approval.

"(10) The use of any false representation or deceptive means to collect or attempt to collect any debt or to obtain information concerning a consumer.

"(11) Except as otherwise provided for communications to acquire location information under section 804, the failure to disclose clearly in all communications made to collect a debt or to obtain information about a consumer, that the debt collector is attempting to collect a debt and that any information obtained will be used for that purpose.

"(12) The false representation or implication that accounts have been turned over to innocent purchasers for value.

"(13) The false representation or implication that documents are legal process.

"(14) The use of any business, company, or organization name other than the true name of the debt collector's business, company, or organization.

"(15) The false representation or implication that documents are not legal process forms or do not require action by the consumer.

"(16) The false representation or implication that a debt collector operates or is employed by a consumer reporting agency as defined by section 603(f) of this Act.

"§808. Unfair practices

"A debt collector may not use unfair or unconscionable means to collect or attempt to collect any debt. Without limiting the general application of the foregoing, the following conduct is a violation of this section:

"(1) The collection of any amount (including any interest, fee, charges, or expense incidental to the

authorized by the agreement creating the debt or permitted by law.

"(2) The acceptance by a debt collector from any person of a check or other payment instrument postdated by more than five days unless such person is notified in writing of the debt collector's intent to deposit such check or instrument not more than ten nor less than three business days prior to such deposit.

"(3) The solicitation by a debt collector of any postdated check or other postdated payment instrument for the purpose of threatening or instituting criminal prosecution.

"(4) Depositing or threatening to deposit any postdated check or other postdated payment instrument prior to the date on such check or instrument.

"(5) Causing charges to be made to any person for communications by concealment of the true purpose of the communication. Such charges include, but are not limited to, collect telephone calls and telegram fees.

"(6) Taking or threatening to take any nonjudicial action to effect dispossession or disablement of property if—

"(A) there is no present right to possession of the property claimed as collateral through an enforceable security interest;

"(B) there is no present intention to take possession of the property; or

"(C) the property is exempt by law from such dispossession or disablement.

"(8) Using any language or symbol, other than the

"(8) Using any language or symbol, other than the debt collector's address, on any envelope when communicating with a consumer by use of the mails or by telegram, except that a debt collector may use his business name if such name does not indicate that he is in the debt collection business.

"§809. Validation of debts

"(a) Within five days after the initial communication with a consumer in connection with the collection of any debt, a debt collector shall, unless the following information is contained in the initial communication or the consumer has paid the debt, send the consumer a written notice containing—

"(1) the amount of the debt;

"(2) the name of the creditor to whom the debt is owed;

"(3) a statement that unless the consumer, within thirty days after receipt of notice, disputes the validity of the debt, or any portion thereof, the debt will be assumed to be valid by the debt collector;

"(4) a statement that if the consumer notifies the debt collector in writing within the thirty-day period that the debt, or any portion thereof, is disputed, the debt collector will obtain verification of the debt or a copy of a judgment against the consumer and a copy of such verification or judgment will be mailed to the consumer by the debt collector; and

"(5) a statement that, upon the consumer's written request within the thirty-day period, the debt collector will provide the consumer with the name and address of the original creditor, if different from the current creditor.

"(b) If the consumer notifies the debt collector in writing within the thirty-day period described in subsection (a) that the debt, or any portion thereof, is disputed, or that the consumer requests the name and address of the original creditor, the debt collector shall cease collection of the debt, or any disputed portion thereof, until the debt collector obtains verification of the debt or a copy of a judgment, or the name and address of the original creditor, and a copy of such verification or judgment, or name and address of the original creditor, is mailed to the consumer by the debt collector.

"(c) The failure of a consumer to dispute the validity of a debt under this section may not be construed by any court as an admission of liability by the consumer.

"§810. Multiple debts

"If any consumer owes multiple debts and makes any single payment to any debt collector with respect to such debts, such debt collector may not apply such payment to any debt which is disputed by the consumer and, where applicable, shall apply such payment in accordance with the consumer's directions.

"§811. Legal actions by debt collectors

"(a) Any debt collector who brings any legal action on a debt against any consumer shall—

"(1) in the case of an action to enforce an interest in real property securing the consumer's obligation, bring such action only in a judicial district or similar legal entity in which such real property is located; or

"(2) in the case of an action not described in paragraph (1), bring such action only in the judicial district or similar legal entity—

"(A) in which such consumer signed the contract sued upon; or

"(B) in which such consumer resides at the commencement of the action.

"(b) Nothing in this title shall be construed to authorize the bringing of legal actions by debt collectors.

"§812. Furnishing certain deceptive forms.

"(a) It is unlawful to design, compile, and furnish any form knowing that such form would be used to create the false belief in a consumer that a person other than the creditor of such consumer is participating in the collection of or in an attempt to collect a debt such consumer allegedly owes such creditor, when in fact such person is not so participating.

"(b) Any person who violates this section shall be liable to the same extent and the same manner as a debt collector is liable under section 813 for failure to comply with a provision of this title.

"§813. Civil liability

"(a) Except as otherwise provided by this section, any debt collector who fails to comply with any provision of this title with respect to any person is liable to such person in an amount equal to the sum of—

"(1) any actual damage sustained by such as a result of such failure;

"(2) (A) in the case of any action by an individual, such additional damages as the court may allow, but not exceeding $1,000; or

each named plaintiff as could be received under subparagraph (A), and (ii) such amount as the court may allow for all other class members, without regard to a minimum individual recovery, not to exceed the lesser of $500,000 or 1 per centum of the net worth of the debt collector; and

"(3) in the case of any successful action to enforce the foregoing liability, the costs of the action, together with a reasonable attorney's fee as determined by the court. On a finding by the court that an action under this section was brought in bad faith and for the purpose of harassment, the court may award to the defendant attorney's fees reasonable in relation to the work expended and cost.

"(b) In determining the amount of liability in any action under subsection (a), the court shall consider, among other relevant factors—

"(1) in any individual action under subsection (a) (2) (A), the frequency and persistence of noncompliance by the debt collector, the nature of such non-compliance, and the extent to which such non-compliance was intentional; or

"(2) in any class action under subsection (a) (2) (B), the frequency and persistence of noncompliance by the debt collector, the nature of such noncompliance, the resources of the debt collector, the number of persons adversely affected, and the extent to which the debt collector's noncompliance was intentional.

"(c) A debt collector may not be held liable in any action brought under this title if the debt collector shows by a

brought under this title if the debt collector shows by a preponderance of evidence that the violation was not intentional and resulted from a bonafide error notwithstanding the maintenance of procedures reasonably adapted to avoid any such error.

"(d) An action to enforce any liability created by this title may be brought in any appropriate United States district court without regard to the amount in controversy, or in another court of competent jurisdiction, within one year from the date on which the violation occurs.

"(e) No provision of this section imposing any liability shall apply to any act done or omitted in good faith in conformity with any advisory opinion of the Commission, not withstanding that after such act or omission has occurred, such opinion is amended, rescinded, or determined by judicial or other authority to be invalid for any reason.

"§814. Administrative enforcement

"(a) Compliance with this title shall be enforced by the Commission, except to the extent that enforcement of the requirements imposed under this title is specifically committed to another agency under subsection (b) For purpose of the exercise by the Commission of its functions and powers under the Federal Trade Commission Act, a violation of this title shall be deemed an unfair or deceptive act or practice in violation of that Act. All of the functions and powers of the Commission under the Federal Trade Commission Act are available to the Commission to enforce compliance by any person with this title, irrespective of whether that person is engaged in commerce or meets any other jurisdictional tests in the Federal Trade Commission

Act, including the power to enforce the provisions of this title in the same manner as if the violation had been violation of a Federal Trade Commision trade regulation rule.

"(b) Compliance with any requirement imposed under this title shall be enforced under—

"(1) section 8 of the Federal Deposit Insurance Act, in the case of—

"(A) national banks, by the Comptroller of the Currency;

"(B) member banks of the Federal Reserve System (other than national banks), by the Federal Reserve Board; and

"(C) banks the deposits or accounts of which are insured by the Federal Deposit Insurance Corporation (other than members of the Federal Reserve System), by the Board of Directors of the Federal Deposit Insurance Corporation;

"(2) section 5(d) of the Home Owners Loan Act of 1933, section 407 of the National Housing Act, and sections 6(i) and 17 of the Federal Home Loan Bank Act, by the Federal Home Loan Bank Board (acting directly or through the Federal Savings and Loan Insurance Corporation) in the case of any institution subject to any of those provisions;

"(3) the Federal Credit Union Act, by the National Credit Union Administration Board with respect to any Federal credit union;

"(4) subtitle IV of Title 49, by the Interstate Commerce Commission with respect to any common carrier subject to such subtitle;

"(5) the Federal Aviation Act of 1958, by the Secretary of Transportation with respect to any air carrier of any foreign air carrier subject to that Act; and

"(6) the Packers and Stockyards Act, 1921 (except as provided in section 406 of that Act, by the Secretary of Agriculture with respect to any activities subject to that Act.

"(c) For the purpose of the exercise by any agency referred to in subsection (b) of its powers under an Act referred to in that subsection, a violation of any requirement imposed under that Act. In addition to its powers under any provision of law specifically referred to in subsection (b), each of the agencies referred to in that subsection may exercise, for the purpose of enforcing compliance with any requirement imposed under this title any other agency referred to in subsection (b) may promulgate trade regulation rules or other regulations with respect to the collection of debt collectors as defined in this title.

"§815. Reports to Congress by the Commission

"(a) Not later than one year after the effective date of this title and at one-year intervals thereafter, the Commission shall make reports to the Congress concerning the administration of its functions under this title, including such recommendations as the Commission deems necessary or appropriate,. In addition, each report of the Commission shall include its assessment of the extent to which compliance with this title is being achieved and a summary of the enforcement actions taken by the Commission under section 814 of this title.

"(b) In the exercise of its functions under this title, the

Commission may obtain upon request the views of any other Federal agency which exercises enforcement functions under section 814 of this title.

"§816. Relation to State laws

"This title does not annul, alter, or affect, or exempt any person subject to the provisions of this title from complying with the laws of any State with respect to debt collection practices, except to the extent that those laws are inconsistent with any provision of this title, and then only to the extent of the inconsistency. For purposes of this section, a State law is not inconsistent with this title if the protection provided by this title.

"§817. Exemption for State regulation

"The Commission shall be regulation exempt from the requirements of this title any class of debt collection practices within any State if the Commission determines that under the law of that State that class of debt collection practices is subject to requirements substantially similar to those imposed by this title, and that there is adequate provision for enforcement.

"§818. Effective date

"This title takes effect upon the expiration of six months after the date of this enactment, but section 809 shall apply only with respect to debts for which the initial attempt to collect occurs after such effective date."

Approved September 20, 1977

LEGISLATIVE HISTORY:

Public Las 95-109 [H.R. 5294]

HOUSE REPORT: No 95-131 (Comm. on Banking, Finance, an Urban Affairs)

SENATE REPORT: No 95-382 (Comm. on Banking, Housing, and Urban Affairs)

CONGRESSIONAL RECORD, Vol. 123 (1977):

Apr. 4, considered and passed House.

Aug. 5, considered and passed Senate, amended.

Sept. 8, House agreed to Senate amendment.

WEEKLY COMPILATION OF PRESIDENTIAL DOCUMENTS, Vol. 13, No. 39:

Sept. 20, Presidential statement.

AMENDMENTS:

SECTION 621, SUBSECTIONS (b) (3), (b) (4) and (b) (5) were amended to transfer certain administrative enforcement responsibilities pursuant to Pub. L. 95-473, / 3(b), Oct. 17, 1978. 92 Stat. 166; Pub. L. 95-630, Title V. 501, November 10, 1978, 92 Stat. 3680; Pub. L. 98-443, 9(h), Oct. 4, 1984, 98 Stat, (708.)

SECTION 803, SUBSECTION (6), defining "debt collector," was amended to repeal the attorney at law exemption at former Section (6) (F) and to redesignate Section 803 (6) (G) pursuant to Pub. L. 99-361, July 9, 1986, 100 Stat. 768. For legislative history, see H.R. 237, HOUSE REPORT No. 99-405 (Comm. on Banking, Finance an Urban Affairs). CONGRESSIONAL RECORD: Vol. 131

(1985): Dec. 2, considered and passed House. Vol. 132
(1986): June 26, considered and passed Senate.

Appendix Z

FEDERAL TRADE COMMISSION REGIONAL OFFICES

Federal Trade Commission
1718 Peachtree St., NW, Room 1000
Atlanta, GA 30367
(covers Alabama, Florida, Georgia, Mississippi,
North Carolina, South Carolina, Tennessee & Virginia)

Federal Trade Commission
150 Causeway St., Room 1301
Boston, MA 02114
(covers Connecticut, Maine, Massachusetts,
New Hampshire, Rhode Island & Vermont)

Federal Trade Commission
55 E. Monroe St., Suite 1437
Chicago, IL 60603
(covers Illinois, Indiana, Iowa, Kentucky,
Minnesota, Missouri & Wisconsin)

Federal Trade Commission
Mall Building, Suite 500
118 St. Clair Avenue
Cleveland, OH 44114
(covers Delaware, Maryland, Michigan,
Ohio, Pennsylvania & West Virginia)

Federal Trade Commission
100 N. Central Expressway, Suite 500
Dallas, TX 75201
(covers Arkansas, Louisiana,
New Mexico, Oklahoma & Texas)

Federal Trade Commission
1405 Curtis St., Suite 2900
Denver, CO 80202
(covers Colorado, Kansas, Montana, Nebraska,

North Dakota, South Dakota, Utah & Wyoming)

Federal Trade Commission
11000 Wilshire Blvd.
Los Angeles, CA 90024

(covers Arizona & Southern California)

Federal Trade Commission
Federal Building, Room 2243-EB
26 Federal Plaza
New York, NY 10278

(cover New Jersey & New York)

Federal Trade Commission
450 Golden Gate Avenue, Room 12470
San Francisco, CA 94102

(covers northern California, Hawaii & Nevada)

Federal Trade Commission
Federal Building, 28th Floor
915 Second Avenue
Seattle, WA 98174

(covers Alaska, Idaho, Oregon & Washington)

Appendix AA

TOP 10 LIST OF CREDIT FACTS FOR CONSUMERS

1. Unless you live in a state with community property laws dictating division/claim of assets and liabilities, prospective creditors cannot inquire about your marital status. Furthermore, prospective creditors cannot inquire about your spouse's income, unless you are claiming both incomes to qualify for a loan.

2. Americans spend over 70% of their gross income every year repaying debt: home loans, auto loans and credit cards.

3. Age discrimination? The actuarial tables know for sure: In the "credit scoring" game, those individuals under the age of 25 score the lowest; prospective debtors in their 40's score highest.

4. Owning a home debt-free doesn't necessarily score any higher than one with a mortgage. The fact that you own your home score positive points when analyzing a prospective debtor.

5. Be aware that if you are self-employed and applying for credit, this can subtract points in the credit scoring game because of inability to verify income, tenure, etc.

6. Credit card companies divide card users into three categories:
   • "Revolvers" those individuals that make the minimum

payment each month;

- •"Average" are those consumers that pay the balance off in full one month and the minimum balance the next;
- •"Convenience users" include those consumers that pay the entire balance every month avoiding interest charges (these are the least profitable to banks).

7. Over 70% of the consumers who use credit cards have no idea what interest rate they are paying on their cards.

8. Unless you have purchased a new car or home in the last 12 months, the chances of your seeing a recent credit report are 1 in 8.

9. Over 90 percent of Americans have no idea what their rights are under federal credit and collections laws.

10. Only 1 in 20 Americans has a current listing on file of all credit card account numbers to refer to in the event of theft or fraud.

Appendix BB

RESOURCES REFERENCE LIST

Bankcard Holders of America: 560 Herndon Parkway, Suite 120, Herndon, VA 22070. Here's two toll-free numbers to reach them: (800) 237-1800 or (800) 553-8025.

Debtors Anonymous: Support groups can be invaluable in your desire to keep on track financially. Write to Debtors Anonymous at P.O. Box 400, Grand Central Station, New York, NY 10163 to find out if there is a chapter near you.

Consumer Fresh Start: If you've already committed the cardinal sin of personal finance and filed for or emerged from a personal bankruptcy, this consumer group provides counseling, support and most importantly ideas on how to get back on your feet. Their address is 217 N. Church Street, Princeton, IL 61356.

Remember, the squeaky wheel gets the grease! If one of these credit card companies is making your life miserable and you really don't deserve it, start at the top!

Call the company in question first to find out the name of the chairman or president (these things change, you know) and send them a certified letter. Results is the name of the game.

American Express
American Express Tower
World Financial Center
200 Vesey St.
New York, NY 10285
(212) 640-2000

Discover Card Services, Inc.
2500 Lake Cook Road, Suite 2-C
Riverwood, IL 60015
(708) 405-0900

MasterCard USA
888 Seventh Avenue
New York, NY 10106
(212) 649-4600

VISA USA, Inc.
3155 Clearview Way
San Mateo, CA 94402
(415) 570-3200

American Collector's Association (ACA): I don't have an enormous amount of faith in this trade association designed to "self-police" the debt collection industry. They'll investigate complaints from consumers, but my best advice is to complain first to the Federal Trade Commission and your state's Attorney General, with a copy of your letters and official complaint copied to the ACA. Here's their address: Post Office Box 35106, Minneapolis, MN 55435.

Consumer Resource Handbook: Published by the U.S. Office of Consumer Affairs, this book is definitely worth the price (free!) and has listings of hundreds of agencies that are there to help consumers with a variety of problems. To get your free copy, write to: The Consumer Resource Handbook, Pueblo, CO 81009.

Appendix CC

SOCIAL SECURITY NUMBERS FACTS

• Anybody applying for an original Social Security Number needs to be prepared to establish their age, identity, citizenship or lawful alien status. Applicants age 18 or older (a real rarity in today's number insistent society) must apply in person. Parents applying for their children's new number should be prepared to show a birth certificate to prove name/age/date of birth/citizenship.

• The system is extremely inefficient when deactivating a Social Security Number upon death. The Social Security Administration depends on information provided by: funeral homes, survivors filing for death benefits, a benefit payment returned by the bank due to the account being closed or returned correspondence from the U.S. Postal Service. The Social Security Administration periodically matches the death records from state vital statistics bureaus with their own records.

• Government agencies can require a person to disclose their Social Security Number only if there is a preexisting law/regulation that requires them to do so. These agencies must tell the person (upon request) what the law/regulation is and the individual has the option to refuse disclosure...of course this raises the possibility of endangering the receipt of the services they were applying for in the first place. Private sector organizations can refuse to offer services if a consumer refuses disclosure of their Social Security Number.

• In order for U.S. citizens to receive proper credit for future Social Security benefits they must have a Social Security Number. This same number is used to track all earnings/withholding information for our friends at the Internal Revenue Service. The Social Security Number is also used as your identifier for the military, state welfare offices and other government agencies.

• Under normal circumstances, your Social Security Number will follow you to your grave. It's extremely difficult to get a new number, and the circumstances must be extraordinary to warrant this action. Religious objections to the number 666 because of the biblical representation as the "sign of the beast", superstition about the number 13, harassment or abuse by an ex-spouse (or others), sequential numbers assigned to members of the same family or two people having the same Social Security Number, resulting in the predictable mass confusion that this could cause. This process is highly unusual and the persona requesting a new number had better be prepared to substantiate their need for a new number. The credit bureaus will "link" the old number to the new number, so don't think you're going to create a new credit identity.

• Federal agencies by law can only disclose information about you/your Social Security Number and any earnings or other data when allowed by law, or forced to by court order. If it is unclear whether if the request does not fall into an easy category, the Freedom of Information Act is referred to for guidance. At this time private sector organizations set their own policy for disclosures, unless specifically restricted by federal law.

- The written consent/release of a Social Security Number holder must be secured before the Social Security Administration will disclose or verify any information.
- The Privacy Act of 1974 specifically cites when information may be released to law enforcement agencies, federal or state program administration (including fraud investigations).

- Knowing or willful use of someone else's Social Security Number is a violation of the Social Security Act and the Department of Justice does prosecute, and result in up to 5 years in prison and a fine of up to $5,000, or both.

- Any evidence of Social Security Number fraud, misuse or abuse should immediately be reported to the director of Health and Human Services at the Social Security Administration office in your area.

Appendix DD

SOCIAL SECURITY NUMBER GEOGRAPHICAL ASSIGNMENTS

001-003	New Hampshire	501-502	N. Dakota
004-007	Maine	503-504	S. Dakota
008-009	Vermont	505-508	Nebraska
010-034	Massachusetts	509-515	Kansas
035-039	Rhode Island	516-517	Montana
040-049	Connecticut	518-519	Idaho
050-134	New York	520	Wyoming
135-158	New Jersey	521-524	Colorado
159-211	Pennsylvania	525	New Mexico
212-220	Maryland	526-527	Arizona
221-222	Delaware	528-529	Utah
223-231	Virginia	530	Nevada
232-236*	West Virginia	531-539	Washington
232	NC/WV	540-544	Oregon
237-246*	North Carolina	545-573	California
247-251	South Carolina	574	Alaska
252-260	Georgia	575-576	Hawaii
261-267	Florida	577-579	D.C.
268-302	Ohio	580*	Virgin Islands
303-317	Indiana	580-584*	Puerto Rico
318-361	Illinois	585	New Mexico
387-399	Wisconsin	586*	Guam
400-407	Kentucky	586*	Am. Samoa
408-415	Tennessee	586*	Philippines
416-424	Alabama	587-588	Mississippi

425-428	Mississippi	589-595	Florida
429-432	Arkansas	596-599	Puerto Rico
433-439	Louisiana	600-601	Arizona
440-448	Oklahoma	602-626	California
449-467	Texas	627-645	Texas
468-477	Minnesota	646-647	Utah
478-485	Iowa	648-649	New Mexico
486-500	Missouri	700-728**	Railroad Board

* Some numbers have been used for multiple states or transferred as needed by the system administrator.

** Reserved for railroad employees. Issuance of numbers in this group was discontinued July, 1963.

Appendix EE

THE EQUAL CREDIT OPPORTUNITY ACT

Public Law 93-495
93rd Congress, H.R.11221
October 28,1974

TITLE V - EQUAL CREDIT OPPORTUNITY

§501. Short Title

This title may be cited as the "Equal Credit Opportunity Act."

§502. Finding and purpose

The Congress finds that there is a need to insure that the various financial institutions and other firms engaged in the extensions of credit exercise their responsibility to make credit available with fairness, impartiality, and without discrimination on the basis of sex or marital status. Economic stabilization would be enhanced and competition among the various financial institutions and other firms engaged in the extension of credit would be strengthened by an absence of discrimination on the basis of sex or marital status, as well as by the informed use of credit which Congress has heretofore sought to promote. It is the purpose of this Act to require that financial institutions and other firms engaged in the extension of credit make that credit equally available to all creditworthy customers without regard to sex or marital status.

§503. Amendment to the consumer Credit Protection Act

The consumer Credit Protection Act (Public Law 90-321), is amended by adding at the end thereof a new title VII:

"TITLE VII—EQUAL CREDIT OPPORTUNITY

"Sec.

"701. Prohibited discrimination.

"702. Definitions.

"703. Regulations.

"704. Administrative enforcement.

"705. Relation to State laws.

"706. Civil liability.

"707. Effective date.

"§701. Prohibited discrimination

"(a) It shall be unlawful for any creditor to discriminate against any applicant on the basis of sex or marital status with respect to any aspect of a credit transaction.

"(b) an inquiry of marital status shall not constitute discrimination for purposes of this title if such inquiry is for the purpose of ascertaining the creditor's rights and remedies applicable to the particular extension of credit, and not to discriminate in a determination of creditworthiness.

"§702. Definitions

"(a) The definitions and rules of construction set forth in this section are applicable for the purposes of this title.

"(b) The term 'applicant' means any person who applies to a creditor directly for an extension, renewal, or continuation of credit, or applies to a creditor indirectly by use of an existing credit plan for an amount exceeding a previously established credit limit.

"(c) The term 'Board' refers to the Board of Governors of the Federal Reserve System.

"(d) The term 'credit' means the right granted by a creditor to a debtor to defer payment of debt or to incur debts and defer its payment or to purchase property or services and defer payment therefore.

"(e) The term 'creditor' means any person who regularly arranges for the extension, renewal, or continuation of credit; or any assignee of an original creditor who participates in the decision to extend, renew, or continue credit.

"(f)) The term 'person' means a natural person, a corporation, government or governmental subdivision agency, trust, estate, partnership, cooperative, or association.

"(g) Any reference to any requirement imposed under this title or any provision thereof includes reference to the regulations of the Board under this title or the provision thereof in question.

"§703. Regulations

"The Board shall prescribe regulations to carry out the purposes of this title. These regulations may contain but are not limited to such classifications, differentiation, or other provision, and may provide for such adjustments and exceptions for any class of transactions, as in the judgment of the Board are necessary or proper to effectuate the purposes of this title, to prevent circumvention or evasion thereof, or to facilitate or substantiate compliance therewith. Such regulations shall be prescribed as soon as possible after the date of enactment of this act, but in no event later than the effective date of this Act.

"§704. Administrative enforcement

"(a) Compliance with the requirements imposed under this title shall be enforced under:

"(1) Section 8 of the Federal Deposit Insurance Act, in the case of

"(A) national banks, by the Comptroller of the Currency,

"(B) member banks of the Federal Reserve System (other than national banks), by the Board,

"(C) banks insured by the Federal Deposit Insurance Corporation (other than members of the Federal Reserve System), by the Board of Directors of the Federal Deposit Insurance Corporation.

"(2) Section 5 (d) of the Home Owners' Loan Act of 1933, section 407 of the National Housing Act, and sections 6 (i) and 17 of the Federal Home Loan Bank Act, by the Federal Home Loan Bank Board (acting directly or through the Federal Savings and Loan Insurance Corporation),in the case of any institution subject to any of those provisions.

"(3) The Federal Credit Union Act, by the Administrator of the National Credit Union Administration with respect to any Federal Credit Union.

"(4) The Acts to regulate commerce, by the Interstate Commerce Commission with respect to any common carrier subject to those Acts.

"(5) The federal Aviation Act of 1958, by the Civil Aeronautics Board with respect to any air carrier or foreign air carrier subject to that Act.

"(6) The packers and Stockyards Act, 1921 (except as provided in section 406 of that Act), by the Secretary of Agriculture with respect to any activities subject to that Act.

"(7) The Farm Credit Act of 1971, by the Farm Credit Administration with respect to any Federal land bank, Federal land bank association, Federal intermediate credit bank, and production credit association;

"(8) The securities Exchange Act of 1934, by the Securities and Exchange Commission with respect to brokers an dealers; and

"(9) The Small Business Investment Act of 1958, by the Small Business Administration, with respect to small business investment companies.

"(b) For the purpose of the exercise by any agency referred to in subsection (a) of its powers under any Act referred to in that subsection, a violation of any requirement imposed under this title shall be deemed to be a violation of a requirement imposed under that Act. In addition to its powers under any provision of law specifically referred to in subsection (a), each of the agencies referred to in that subsection may exercise for the purpose of enforcing compliance with any requirement imposed under this title, any other authority conferred on it by law. The exercise of the authorities of any of the agencies referred to in subsection (a) for the purpose of enforcing compliance with any requirement imposed under this title shall in no way preclude the exercise of such authorities for the purpose of enforcing compliance with any other provision of law not relating to the prohibition of discrimination on the basis of sex or marital status with respect to any aspect of a credit transaction.

"(c) Except to the extent that enforcement of the requirements imposed under this title is specifically committed to some other Government agency under subsection (a), the Federal Trade Commission shall enforce such requirements. For the purpose of the exercise by the Federal Trade Commission Act, a violation of any requirement imposed under this title shall be deemed a violation of a requirement imposed under that Act. All of the functions and powers of the Federal Trade Commission under the Federal Trade Commission Act are available to the Commission to enforce compliance by any person with the requirements imposed under this title, irrespective of whether that person is engaged in commerce or meets any other jurisdictional tests in the Federal Trade Commission Act.

"(d) The authority of the Board to issue regulations under this title does not impair the authority of any other agency designated in this section to make rules respecting its own procedures in enforcing compliance with requirements imposed under this title.

"§705. Relation to State laws

"(a) A request for the signature of both parties to a marriage for the purpose of creating valid lien, passing clear title, waiving inchoate rights to property, or assigning earnings, shall not constitute discrimination under this title; Provided, however, that this provision shall not be construed to permit a creditor to take sex or marital status into account in connection with the evaluation of creditworthiness of any applicant.

"(b) Consideration or application of State property laws directly or indirectly affecting creditworthiness shall not constitute discrimination for purposes of this title.

"(c) Any provision of State law which prohibits the separate extension of consumer credit to each party to a marriage shall not apply in any case where each party to a marriage voluntarily applies for separate credit from the same creditor: Provided, That in any case where such a State law is so preempted, each party to the marriage shall be solely responsible for the debt so contracted.

"(d) When each party to a marriage separately and voluntarily applies for and obtains separate credit accounts with the same creditor, those accounts shall not be aggregated or otherwise combined for purposes of determining permissible finance charges or permissible finance charges or permissible loan ceilings under the laws of any State or of the United States.

"(e) Except as otherwise provided in this title, the applicant shall have the option of pursuing remedies under the provisions of this title in lieu of, but not in addition to, the remedies provided by the laws of any State or governmental subdivision relating to the prohibition of discrimination on the basis of sex or marital status with respect to any aspect of a credit transaction.

"§706. Civil liability

"(a) Any creditor who fails to comply with any requirement imposed under this title shall be liable to the aggrieved applicant in an amount equal to the sum of any actual damages sustained by such applicant acting eight in an individual capacity or as a representative of a class.

"(b) Any creditor who fails to comply with any require-ment imposed under this title shall be liable to the aggrieved applicant for punitive damages in an amount not greater than $10,000, as determined by the court, in addition to any actual damages provided in section 706 (a): Provided, how-ever, That in pursuing the recovery allowed under this subsection, the applicant may proceed only in an individual capacity and not as a representative of a class.

"(c) Section 706 (b) notwithstanding, any creditor who fails to comply with any requirement imposed under this title may he liable for punitive damages in the case of a class action in such amount as the court may allow, except that as to each member of the class no minimum recovery shall be applicable, and the total recovery in such action shall not exceed the lesser of $100,,000 or 1 percent of the net worth of the creditor. In determining the amount of award in any class action, the court shall consider, among other relevant factors, the amount of any actual damages awarded, the frequency and persistence of failures of com-pliance by the creditor, the resources of the creditor, the number of persons adversely affected, and the extent to which the creditor's failure of compliance was intentional.

"(d) When a creditor fails to comply with any require-ment imposed under this title, an aggrieved applicant may institute a civil action for preventive relief, including an application for a permanent or temporary injunction, re-straining order, or other action.

"(e) In the case of any successful action to enforce the foregoing liability, the costs of the action, together with a reasonable attorney's fee as determined by the court shall be added to any damages awarded by the court under the provisions of subsections (a), (b), and (c) of this section.

"(f) No provision of this title imposing any liability shall apply to any act done or omitted in good faith in conformity with any rule, regulation, or interpretation thereof by the Board, notwithstanding that after such act or omission has occurred, such rule, regulation, or interpretation is amended, rescinded, or determined by judicial or other authority to be invalid for any reason.

"(g) Without regard to the amount in controversy, any action under this title may be brought in any United States district court, or in any other court of competent jurisdiction, within one year from the date of the occurrence of the violation.

"§707. Effective date

"This title takes effect upon the expiration of one year after the date of its enactment."

Public Law 94-239
94th Congress, H.R. 6516
March 23, 1976

AN ACT

To amend title VII of the Consumer Credit Protection Act to include discrimination on the basis of race, color, religion, national origin, and age, and for other purposes.

tives of the United States of America in Congress assembled. That (a) this Act may be cited as the "Equal Credit Opportunity Act Amendments of 1976."

(b) Title VII of the Consumer Credit Protection Act is amended by adding at the end thereof the following new section:

"§709. Short Title

"This title may be cited as the 'Equal Credit Opportunity Act.'"

(c) Section 501 of Public Law 93—495 is repealed.

Sec. 2 Section 701 of the Equal Credit Opportunity Act is amended to read as follows:

"§701. Prohibited discrimination; reasons for adverse action

"(a) It shall be unlawful for any creditor to discriminate against any applicant, with respect to any aspect of a credit transaction—

"(1) on the basis of race, color, religion, national origin, sex or marital status, or age (provided the applicant has the capacity to contract):

"(2) because all or part of the applicant's income derives from any public assistance program: or

"(3) because the applicant has in good faith exercised any right under the Consumer Credit Protection Act.

"(b) It shall not constitute discrimination for purposes of this title for a creditor—

"(1) to make an inquiry of marital status if such inquiry is for the purpose of ascertaining the creditor's rights and remedies applicable to the particular exten-

rights and remedies applicable to the particular extension of credit and not to discriminate in a determination of credit-worthiness;

"(2) to make an inquiry of the applicant's age or of whether the applicant's income derives from any public assistance program if such inquiry is for the purpose of determining the amount and probable continuance of income levels, credit history, or other pertinent element of credit-worthiness as provided in regulations of the Board:

"(3) to use any empirically derived credit system which considers age if such system is demonstrably and statistically sound in accordance with regulations of the Board, except that in the operation of such system of the age of an elderly applicant may not be assigned a negative factor or value; or

"(4) to make an inquiry or to consider the age of an elderly applicant when the age of such applicant is to be used by the creditor in the extension of credit in favor of such applicant.

"(c) It is not a violation of this section for a creditor to refuse to extend credit offered pursuant to—

"(1) any credit assistance program expressly authorized by law for an economically disadvantaged class of persons:

"(2) any credit assistance program administered by a nonprofit organization for its members or an economically disadvantaged class of persons; or

"(3) any special purpose credit program offered by a profitmaking organization to meet special social needs which meets standards prescribed in regulations by the

Board: if such refusal is required by or made pursuant to such program.

"(d) (1) Within thirty days (or such longer reasonable time as specified in regulations of the Board for any class of credit transaction) after receipt of a completed application for credit, a creditor shall notify the applicant of its action on the application.

"(2) Each applicant against whom adverse action is taken shall be entitled to a statement of reasons for such action from the creditor. A creditor satisfies this obligation by—

"(A) providing statements of reasons in writing as a matter of course to applicants against whom adverse action is taken; or

"(B) giving written notification of adverse action which discloses (i) the applicant's right to a statement of reasons within thirty days after receipt by the creditor of a request made within sixty days after such notification, and (ii) the identity of the person or office from which such statement may be obtained. Such statement may be given orally if the written notification advises the applicant of his right to have the statement of reasons confirmed in writing on written request.

"(3) A statement of reasons meets the requirements of this section only if it contains the specific reasons for the adverse action taken.

"(4) Where a creditor has been requested by a third party to make a specific extension of credit directly or indirectly to an applicant, the notification and statement of reasons required by this subsection may be made directly by such creditor, or indirectly through the third party, provided in either case that the identity of the creditor is disclosed.

"(5) The requirements of paragraph (2), (3), or (4) may be satisfied by verbal statements or notifications in the case of any creditor who did not act on more that one hundred and fifty applications during the calendar year preceding the calendar year in which the adverse action is taken, as determined under regulations of the Board.

"(6) For purposes of this subsection, the term 'adverse action' means a denial or revocation of credit, a change in the terms of an existing credit arrangement, or a refusal to grant credit in substantially the amount or on substantially the terms requested. Such tern does not include a refusal to extend additional credit under an existing credit arrangement where the applicant is delinquent or otherwise in default, or where such additional credit would exceed a previously established credit limit."

Sec. 3. (a) Section 703 of the Equal Credit Opportunity Act is amended

(1) by inserting "(a)" immediately before "The Board":

(2) by inserting after the second sentence thereof the following new sentence: "In particular, such regulations may exempt from one or more of the provisions of this title any class of transactions not primarily for personal, family, or household purposes., if the Board makes an express finding that the application of such provision or provisions would not contribute substantially to carrying out the purposes of this title"; and

(3) by adding at the end thereof the following new subsection:

"(b) The Board shall establish a Consumer Advisory

Council to advise and consult with it in the exercise of its functions under the Consumer Credit Protection Act and to advise and consult with it concerning other consumer related matters it may place before the Council. In appointing the members of the Council, the Board shall seek to achieve a fair representation of the interests of creditors and consumers. The Council shall meet from time to time at the call of the Board. Members of the Council who are not regular full-time employees of the United States shall, while attending meetings of such Council, be entitled to receive compensation at a rate fixed by the Board, but not exceeding $100 per day, including travel time. Such members may be allowed travel expenses, including transportation and subsistence, while away from their homes or regular place of business."

(b) (1) Section 110 of the Truth in Lending Act is repealed.

(2) The table of sections of chapter 1 of such Act is amended by striking out item 110.

SEC. 4. Section 704 (c) of the Equal Credit Opportunity Act is amended by inserting before the period at the end thereof the following: "including the power to enforce any Federal Reserve Board regulation promulgated under this title in the same manner as if the violation had been a violation of a Federal Trade Commission trade regulation rule".

SEC. 5. Section 705 of the Equal Credit Opportunity Act is amended

(1) by amending subsection (e) to read as follows:

"(e) Where the same act or omission constitutes a violation of this title and of applicable State law, a person aggrieved by such conduct may bring a legal action to recover monetary damages either under this title or under such State law, but not both. This election of remedies shall not apply to court actions in which the relief sought does not include monetary damages or to administrative actions."; and

(2) by adding the following new subsections:

"(f) This title does not annul, alter, or affect, or exempt any person subject to the provisions of this title from complying with, the laws of any State with respect to credit discrimination, except to the extent that those laws are inconsistent with any provision of this title if the Board determines that such law gives greater protection to the applicant.

"(g) The Board shall by regulation exempt from the requirements of sections 701 and 702 of this title any class of credit transactions within any State if it determines that under the law of that State that class of transactions is subject to requirements substantially similar to those imposed under this title or that such law gives greater protection to the applicant, and that there is adequate provision for enforcement. Failure to comply with any requirement of such State law in any transaction so exempted shall constitute a violation of this title for the purposes of section 705.".

SEC. 6 Section 706 of the Equal Credit Opportunity Act is amended to read as follows:

"§706. Civil liability

"(a) Any creditor who fails to comply with any requirement imposed under this title shall be liable to the aggrieved applicant for any actual damages sustained by such appli-

of a class-action lawsuit.

"(b) Any creditor, other than a government or governmental subdivision or agency, who fails to comply with any requirement imposed under this title shall be liable to the aggrieved applicant for punitive damages in an amount not greater than $10,000, in addition to any actual damages provided in subsection (a), except that in the case of a class action the total recovery under this subsection shall not exceed the lesser of $500,000 or 1 per centum of the net worth of the creditor. In determining the amount of such damages in any action, the court shall consider, among other relevant factors, the amount of any actual damages awarded, the frequency and persistence of failures of compliance by the creditor, the resources of the creditor, the number of persons adversely affected, and the extent to which the creditor's failure of compliance was intentional.

"(c) Upon application by an aggrieved applicant, the appropriate United States district court or any other court of competent jurisdiction may grant such equitable and declaratory relief as is necessary to enforce the requirements imposed under this title.

"(d) In the case of any successful action under subsection (a), (b), or (c), the costs of the action, together with a reasonable attorney's fee as determined by the court, shall be added to any damages awarded by the court under such subsection.

"(e) No provision of this title imposing liability shall apply to any act done or omitted in good faith in conformity with any official rule, regulation, or interpretation thereof by the Board or in conformity with any interpretation or

by the Board or in conformity with any interpretation or approval by an official or employee of the Federal Reserve System duly authorized by the Board to issue such interpretations or approvals under such procedures as the Board may prescribe therefor, notwithstanding that after such act or omission has occurred, such rule, regulation, interpretation, or approval is amended, rescinded, or determined by judicial or other authority to be invalid for any reason.

"(f) Any action under this section may be brought in the appropriate United States district court without regard to the amount in controversy, or in any other court of competent jurisdiction. No such action shall be brought later than two years from the date of the occurrence of the violation, except that

"(1) whenever any agency having responsibility for administrative enforcement under section 704 commences an enforcement proceeding within two years from the date of the occurrence of the violation.

"(2) whenever the Attorney General commences a civil action under this section within two years from the date of the occurrence of the violation,

then any applicant who has been a victim of the discrimination which is the subject of such proceeding or civil action may bring an action under this section not later than one year after the commencement of that proceeding or action.

"(g) The agencies having responsibility for administrative enforcement under section 704, if unable to obtain compliance with section 701, are authorized to refer the matter to the Attorney General with recommendation that an appropriate civil action be instituted.

"(h) When a matter is referred to the Attorney General pursuant to subsection

"(g), or whenever he has reason to believe that one or more creditors are engaged in a pattern or practice in violation of this title, the Attorney General may bring a civil action in any appropriate United States district court for such relief as may be appropriate, including injunctive relief.

"(i) No person aggrieved by a violation of this title and by a violation of section 805 of the Civil Rights Act of 1968 shall recover under this title and section 812 of the Civil Rights Act of 1968, it such violation is based on the same transaction.

"(j) Nothing in this title shall be construed to prohibit the discovery of a creditor's credit granting standards under appropriate discovery procedures in the court or agency in which an action or proceeding is brought.".

SEC. 7 The Equal Credit Opportunity Act is amended by redesignating section 707 as section 708 and by inserting immediately after section 706 the following new section:

"§707. Annual reports to Congress

"Not later than February 1 of each year after 1976, the Board and the Attorney General shall, respectively, make reports to the Congress concerning the administration of their functions under this title, including such recommendations as the Board and the Attorney General, respectively, deem necessary or appropriate. In addition, each report of the Board shall include its assessment of the extent to which compliance with the requirements of this title is being achieved, and a summary of the enforcement actions taken by each of the agencies assigned administrative enforcement responsibilities under section 704.".

SEC. 8. Section 708 of the Equal Credit Opportunity Act is amended by adding at the end thereof the following new sentence: "The amendments made by the Equal Credit Opportunity Act Amendments of 1976 shall take effect on the date of enactment thereof and shall apply to any violation occurring on or after such date, except that the amendments made to section 701 of the Equal Credit Opportunity Act shall take effect 12 months after the date of enactment."

SEC. 9. The table of sections of the Equal Credit Opportunity Act is amended by striking out:

"707. Effective date."

and inserting in lieu thereof the following new items.

"707. Annual reports to Congress.

"708 Effective date.

"709. Short title."

Approved March 23, 1976.

LEGISLATIVE HISTORY:

HOUSE REPORTS: No. 94-210 (Comm. on Banking, Currency and Housing) and
No. 94- 873 (Comm. of conference),
SENATE REPORT: No 94-589 (Comm. on Banking, Housing and Urban Affairs).

CONGRESSIONAL RECORD:

Vol. 121 (1975): June 3, considered and passed House.

Vol. 122 (1976): Feb. 2 considered and passed Senate, amended,

Mar. 9, Senate and House agreed to conference report.

WEEKLY COMPILATION OF PRESIDENTIAL DOCUMENTS:

Vol. 12, no. 13 (1976): Mar 23, Presidential statement.

Appendix FF

THE FAIR CREDIT BILLING ACT

Public Law 93-495
93rd Congress, H. r. 11221
October 28, 1974

TITLE III—FAIR CREDIT BILLING

§301. Short title

This title may be cited as the "Fair Credit Billing Act".

§302. Declaration of purpose

The last sentence of section 102 of the Truth in Lending Act (15 U.S.C. 1601) is amended by striking out the period and inserting in lieu thereof a comma and the following: "and to protect the consumer against inaccurate and unfair credit billing and credit card practices."

§303. Definitions of creditor and open end credit plan

The first sentence of section 103 (f) of the Truth in Lending Act (15 U.S.C. 1602(f) in amended to read as follows: "The term 'creditor' refers only to creditors who regularly extend, or arrange for the extension of, credit which is payable by agreement in more than four installments or for which the payment of a finance charge is or may be required, whether in connection with loans, sales of property or services, or otherwise. For the purposes of the requirements imposed under Chapter 4 and sections 127 (a) (6), 127 (a) (7), 127 (a) (8), 127 (b) (1), 127 (b) (2), 127 (b) (3), 127 (b) (9), and 127 (b) (11) of Chapter 2 of this Title, the term 'creditor' shall also include card issuers whether or not the amount due is payable by agreement in more than four installments or the payment of a finance charge is or may be required, and the Board shall, by regulation, apply these requirements to such card issuers, to the extent appropriate, even though the requirements are by their terms applicable only to creditors offering open end credit plans.

§304. Disclosure of fair credit billing rights

(a) Section 127 (a) of the Truth in Lending Act (15 U.S.C. 1637(a) is amended by adding t the end thereof a new paragraph as follows:

"(8) A statement, in a form prescribed by regulations of the Board of the protection provided by sections 161 and 170 to an obligor and the creditor's responsibilities under sections 162 and 170. With respect to each of two billing cycles per year, at semiannual intervals, the creditor shall transmit such statement to each obligor to whom the creditor is required to transmit a statement pursuant to section 127 (b) for such billing cycle."

(b) Section 127 (c) of such Act (15 U.S.C. 1637 (c) is amended to read:

"(c) In the case of any existing account under an open end consumer credit plan having an outstanding balance of more than $1 at or after the close of the creditor's first full billing cycle under the plan after the effective date of subsection (a), to the extent applicable and not previously disclosed, shall be disclosed in a notice mailed or delivered to the obligor not later than the time of mailing the next statement required by subsection(b)."

§305. Disclosure of billing contact

Section 127 (b) of the Truth in Lending Act (15 U.S.C. 1637 (b) is amended by adding at the end thereof a new paragraph as follows:

"(11)The address to be used by the creditor for the purpose of receiving billing inquiries from the obligor."

§306. Billing practices

The Truth in Lending Act (15 U.S.C. 1601-1665) is amended by adding at the end thereof a new chapter as follows:

CHAPTER 4 - CREDIT BILLING

"Sec.

"161. Correction of billing errors.
"162. Regulation of credit reports.
"163. Length of billing period.
"164. Prompt crediting of payments.
"165. Crediting excess payments.
"166. Prompt notification of returns.
"167. Use of cash discounts.
"168. Prohibition of tie-in services.
"169. Prohibition of offsets.
"170. Rights of credit card customers.
"171. Relation to State laws.

"§161. Correction of billing errors

"(a) If a creditor, within sixty days after having transmitted to an obligor a statement of the obligor's account in connection with an extension of consumer credit, receives at the address disclosed under section 127 (b) (11) a written notice (other than notice on a payment stub or other payment medium supplied by the creditor if the creditor so stipulates with the disclosure required under section 127 (a) (8) from the obligor in which the obligor—

"(1) sets forth or otherwise enables the creditor to identify the name and account number (if any) of the obligor,

"(2) indicates the obligor's belief that the statement contains a billing error and the amount of such billing error, and extent applicable) that the statement contains a billing error, the creditor shall, unless the obligor has, after giving such written notice and before the expiration of the time limits herein specified, agreed that the statement was correct—

"(3) sets forth the reasons for the obligor's belief (to the extent applicable) that the statement contains a billing error, the creditor shall, unless the obligor has, after giving such written notice and before the expiration of the time limits herein specified. agreed that the statement was correct—

"(A) not later than thirty days after the receipt of the notice, send a written acknowledgment thereof to the obligor, unless the action required in subparagraph (B) is taken within such thirty-day period, and

"(B) not later than two complete billing cycles of the creditor (in no event later than ninety days) after the receipt of the notice and prior to taking any action to collect the amount, or any part thereof, indicated by the obligor under paragraph (2) either—

"(i) make appropriate corrections in the account of the obligor, including the crediting of any finance charges on amounts erroneously billed, and transmit to the obligor a notification of such corrections and the creditor's explanation of any change in the amount indicated by the obligor under paragraph (2) and, if any such change is made and the obligor so requests, copies of documentary evidence of the obligor's indebtedness; or

"(ii) send a written explanation or clarification to the obligor, after having conducted an investigation, setting forth to the extent applicable the reasons why the creditor believes the account of the obligor was correctly shown in the statement and, upon request of the obligor, provide copies of documentary evidence of the obligor's indebtedness. In the case of a billing error where the obligor alleges that the creditor's billing statement reflects goods not delivered to the obligor or his designee in accordance with the agreement made at the time of the transaction, a creditor may not construe such amount to be correctly shown unless he determines that such goods were actually delivered, mailed, or otherwise sent to the obligor and provides the obligor with a statement of such determination.

After complying with the provisions of this subsection with respect to an alleged billing error, a creditor has no further responsibility under this section if the obligor continues to make substantially the same allegation with respect to such error.

"(b) For the purpose of this section, a 'billing error' consists of any of the following:

"(1) A reflection on a statement of an extension of

credit which was not make to the obligor, or, if made, was not in the amount reflected on such statement.

"(2) A reflection on a statement of an extension of credit for which the obligor requests additional clarification including documentary evidence thereof.

"(3) A reflection on a statement of goods or services not accepted by the obligor or his designee or not delivered to the obligor or his designee in accordance with the agreement made at the time of a transaction.

"(4) The creditor's failure to reflect properly on a statement a payment made by the obligor or a credit issued tot he obligor.

"(5) A computation error or similar error of an accounting nature of the creditor on a statement.

"(6) Any other error described in regulations of the Board.

"(c) For the purposes of this section, 'action to collect the amount or any part thereof, indicated by an obligor under paragraph (2)' does not include the sending of statements of account to the obligor following written notice from the obligor as specified under subsection (a), if—

"(1) the obligor's account is not restricted or closed because of the failure of the obligor to pay the amount indicated under paragraph (2) of subsection (a), and

"(2) the creditor indicates the payment of such amount is not required pending the creditor's compliance with this section.

Nothing in this section shall be construed to prohibit any action by a creditor to collect any amount which has not been indicated by the obligor to contain a billing error.

"(d) Pursuant to regulations of the Board, a creditor operating an open end consumer credit plan may not, prior to the sending of the written explanation or clarification required under paragraph (B) (ii), restrict or close an account with respect to which the obligor has indicated pursuant to subsection (a) that he believes such account to contain a billing error solely because of the obligor's failure to pay the amount indicated to be in error. Nothing in this subsection shall be deemed to prohibit a creditor from applying against the credit limit on the obligor's account the amount indicated to be in error.

"(e) Any creditor who fails to comply with the requirements of this section or section 162 forfeits any right to collect from the obligor the amount indicated by the obligor under paragraph (2) of subsection (a) of this section, and any finance charges thereon, except that the amount required to be forfeited under this subsection may not exceed $50.

"§162. Regulation of credit reports

"(a) After receiving a notice from an obligor as provided in section 161 (a), a creditor or his agent may not directly or indirectly threaten to report to any person adversely on the obligor's credit rating or credit standing because of the obligor's failure to pay the amount indicated by the obligor under section 161 (a) (2), and such amount may not be reported as delinquent to any third party until the creditor has met the requirements of section 161 and has allowed the obligor the same number of days (not less than ten) thereafter to make payment a is provided under the credit agreement with the obligor for the payment of undisputed

"(b) If a creditor receives a further written notice from an obligor that an amount is still in dispute within the time allowed for payment under subsection (a) of this section, a creditor may not report to any third party that the amount of the obligor is delinquent because the obligor has failed to pay an amount which he has indicated under section 161 (a) (2), unless the creditor also reports that the amount is in dispute and, at the same time, notifies the obligor of the name and address of each party to whom the creditor is reporting information concerning the delinquency.

"(c) A creditor shall report any subsequent resolution of any delinquencies reported pursuant to subsection (b) to the parties to whom such delinquencies were initially reported.

"§163. Length of billing period

"(a) If an open end consumer credit plan provides a time period within which an obligor may repay any portion of credit extended without incurring an additional finance charge, such additional finance charge may not be imposed with respect to such portion of the credit extended for the billing cycle of which such period is a part unless a statement which includes the amount upon which the finance charge for that period is based was mailed at least fourteen days prior to the date specified in the statement by which payment must be made in order to avoid imposition of that finance charge.

"(b) Subsection (a) does not apply in any case where a creditor has been prevented, delayed, or hindered in making timely mailing or delivery of such statement within the time period specified in such subsection because

within the time period specified in such subsection because of an act of God, war, natural disaster, strike, or other excusable or justifiable cause, as determined under regulations of the Board.

"§164. Prompt crediting of payments

"Payments received from an obligor under an open end consumer credit plan by the creditor shall be posted promptly to the obligor's account as specified in regulations of the Board, Such regulations shall prevent a finance charge from being imposed on any obligor if the creditor has received the obligor's payment in readily identifiable form in the amount, manner, location, and time indicated by the creditor to avoid the imposition thereof.

"§165. Crediting excess payments

"Whenever an obligor transmits funds to a creditor in excess of the total balance due on an open end consumer credit account, the creditor shall promptly (1) upon request of the obligor refund the amount of the overpayment, or (2) credit such amount to the obligor's account.

"§166. Prompt notification of returns

"with respect to any sales transaction where a credit card has been used to obtain credit, where the seller is a person other than the card issuer, and where the seller accepts or allows a return of the goods or forgiveness of a debit for services which were the subject of such sale, the seller shall promptly transmit to the credit card issuer, a credit statement with respect thereto and the credit card issuer shall credit the account of the obligor for the amount of the transaction.

"§167. Use of cash discounts

"(a) With respect to credit card which may be used for extensions of credit in sales transactions in which the seller is a person other than the card issuer, the card issuer may not, by contract or otherwise, prohibit any such seller from offering a discount to a cardholder to induce the cardholder to pay by cash, check, or similar means rather than use a credit card.

"(b) With respect to any sales transaction, any discount not in excess of 5 per centum offered by the seller for the purpose of inducing payment by cash, check, or other means not involving the use of a credit card shall constitute a finance charge as determined under section 106m if such discount is offered to all prospective buyers and its availability is disclosed to all prospective buyers clearly and conspicuously in accordance with regulations of the Board.

"§168. Prohibition of tie-in services

"Notwithstanding any agreement to the contrary, a card issuer may not require a seller, as a condition to participating in a credit card plan, to open an account with or procure any other service from the card issuer or its subsidiary or agent.

"§169. Prohibition of offsets

"(a) A card issuer may not take any action to offset a cardholder's indebtedness arising in connection with a consumer credit transaction under the relevant credit card plan against funds of the cardholder held on deposit with the card issuer unless—

"(1) such action was previously authorized in writing

by the cardholder in accordance with a credit plan whereby the cardholder agrees periodically to pay debts incurred in his open end credit account by permitting the card issuer periodically to deduct all or a portion of such debt from the cardholder's deposit account,
and

"(2) such action with respect to any outstanding disputed amount not be taken by the card issuer upon request of the cardholder.
In the case of any credit card account in existence on the effective date of this section, the previous written authorization referred to in clause (1) shall not be required until the date (after such effective date) when such account is renewed, but in no case later than one year after such effective date. Such written authorization shall be deemed to exist if the card issuer has previously notified the cardholder that the use of his credit card account will subject any funds which the card issuer holds in deposit accounts of such cardholder to offset against any amounts due and payable on his credit card account which have not been paid in accordance with the terms of the agreement between the card issuer and the cardholder.

"(b) This section does not alter or affect the right under State law of a card issuer to attach or otherwise levy upon funds of a cardholder held on deposit with the card issuer if that remedy is constitutionally available to creditors generally.

"§170. Rights of credit card customers

"(a) Subject to the limitation contained in subsection (b), a card issuer who has issued a credit card to a cardholder pursuant to an open end consumer credit plan shall be subject to all claims (other than tort claims) and defenses arising out of any transaction in which the credit card is used as a method of payment or extension of credit if (1) the obligor has made a good faith attempt to obtain satisfactory resolution of a disagreement or problem relative to the transaction from the person honoring the credit card; (2) the amount of the initial transaction exceeds $50; and (3) the place where the initial transaction occurred was in the same State as the mailing address previously provided by the cardholder or was within 100 miles from such address, except that the limitations set forth in clauses (2) and (3) with respect to an obligor's right to assert claims and defenses against a card issuer shall not be applicable to any transaction in which the person honoring the credit card (A) is the same person as the card issuer, (B) is controlled by the card issuer, (C) is under direct or indirect common control with the card issuer, (D) is a franchised dealer in the card issuer's products or services, or (E) had obtained the order for such transaction through a mail solicitation made by or participated in by the card issuer in which the cardholder is solicited to enter into such transaction by using the credit card issued by the card issuer.

"(b) The amount of claims or defenses asserted by the cardholder may not exceed the amount of credit outstanding with respect to such transaction at the time the cardholder first notifies the card issuer of the person honoring the credit card of such claim or defense. For the purpose of determining the amount of credit outstanding in the preceding sentence, payments and credits to the cardholder's account are deemed to have been applied, in the order indicated, to the payment of: (1) late charges in the order of their entry to the account; (2) finance charges in order of their entry to the account;and (3) debits to the account other than those set forth above, in the order in which each debit entry to the account was made.

"§171. Relation to Sate laws

"(a) This chapter does not annul, alter, or affect, or exempt any person subject to the provisions of this chapter from complying with, the laws of any state with respect to credit billing practices, except to the extent that those laws are inconsistent with any provision of this chapter if the Board determines that such law gives greater protection to the consumer.

"(b) The Board shall by regulation exempt from the requirements of his chapter any class of credit transactions within any State if it determines that under the law of that State that class of transactions is subject to requirements substantially similar to those imposed under this chapter or that such law gives greater protection to the consumer, and that there is adequate provision for enforcement."

"§307. Conforming amendments

(a) The table of chapters of the Truth in Lending Act is amended by adding immediately under item 3 the following:

"4. CREDIT BILLING...161"

(b)Section 11 (d) of such Act (15 U.S.C. 1610 (d) is amended by striking out "and 130" and inserting in lieu thereof a comma and the following: "130, and 166".

(c) Section 121 (a) of such Act (15 U.S.C.. 1610 (d) is amended—

(1) by striking out "and upon whom a finance charge is or may be imposed"; and

(2) by inserting "or chapter 4" immediately after "this chapter".

(d) Section 121 (b) of such Act (15 U.S.C. 1631 (b)) is amended by inserting "or chapter 4" immediately after "this chapter".

(e) Section 122 (a) of such Act (15 US.C. 1632 (a)) is amended by inserting "or chapter 4" immediately after "this chapter".

(f) Section 122 (b) of such Act (15 U.S.C. 1632 (b)) is amended by inserting "or chapter 4" immediately after "this chapter".

§308. Effective date

This title takes effect upon the expiration of one year after the date of its enactment.

Glossary

Accounts Receivable: Term used for credit extended by any person or company to another normally unsecured, with usual repayment terms requiring a monthly payment to amortize the balance owed.

Amortize: To liquidate or reduce an amount owed through a series of payments.

Attorney: A legal agent authorized to appear before a court of law as a representative of a party to a legal controversy.

Autodata: Type of reporting system used by the majority of creditors to grade the payment history of debtors/consumers. Normally updated on a quarterly basis and forwarded to the major credit reporting bureaus on computer tape, these entries can be the most difficult to keep permanently off of a credit report.

Bad Debt Expense: An accounting category reserved for debts deemed uncollectible.

Blackmail: Any payment induced by or through intimidation, by use of threats of injurious information or accusations. (A technique frequently used by unethical debt collection agencies.)

Certified Mail: Specialized postal service technique utilized to track delivery and obtain proof of delivery of letters or packages.

Charge-off: Term used by creditors to describe action taken on an uncollectible account. Alternative term used: *Written Off To Bad Debt Expense.* This action normally results in negative information lines on a credit report that can stay for at least 7 years.

Class-action lawsuit: A legal action initiated by 3 or more parties against a defendant. Many suits in this category are initiated by state or federal attorneys.

Coercion: Exercising force to obtain compliance. A favorite technique employed by debt collectors and attorneys representing creditors.

Commission: A sum or percentage paid to a person for his successful completion of services.

Consumer friendly: Term used frequently to describe ease of understanding of a file or report. Many times this is false and is more of a product of a corporation's public relations department.

Consumer literacy test: A test proposed by the author to be given to high school students to determine competency in basic consumer skills. These skills include how to open checking and savings accounts, how to balance a checkbook, how to create/follow a budget, how credit cards work, a brief understanding of insurance, etc.

Contingency Basis: A fee paid to a third party for their involvement in either a legal proceeding or debt collection.

This fee is normally paid only when a successful outcome to a legal proceeding or debt has been collected, either in part or in full.

Credit grantors: Companies or individuals that extend financing to consumers. A credit grantor can be a mortgage company willing to finance a house, a bank willing to finance an automobile, or a major national credit grantor willing to extend credit through the issuance of a charge card such as Visa, MasterCard or Discover.

Credit manager: Individual that oversees the lending department in a bank, department store or other credit granting entity. Many times this individual will work closely with the collections manager to develop collections strategies of past due/bad debts.

Credit record: National grading system filed by subject's name, birth date and social security number. Major companies providing these services include TRW, Trans Union and Equifax.

Credit repair manual: Derogatory term used by the credit reporting industry for any books that may show consumers the inside information about their industry.

Death alert: A tagline of information originated by the Department of Health and Human Services and distributed to the credit reporting agencies notifying them that a social security number is no longer valid due to the death of the person that belongs to that number. A useful tool to combat credit fraud against lenders.

Deep Discounts: Selling Accounts Receivable or Bad Debts at an amount normally less than 50% of the outstanding balance.

Defaulted student loans: Loans made to students to attend secondary educational institutions at low interest rates. These were guaranteed by the federal government as an inducement to banks to make these loans but as a result, were poorly researched before being made. Over $13 billion of these loans exist and are now owned by the U.S. government.

Deferments: Contractually agreed to period of time a borrower is allowed to suspend payment on a debt. Usually applies to student loans and suspends the accrual of interest or late fees on the outstanding loan balance.

Depositions: Sworn statements made in the presence of a court reporter (usually) as a result of questions posed by attorneys in court (or post judgment) action. These statements are normally made outside a court of law, but are fully admissible during trial and fully binding under perjury statutes.

Discharged: To relieve of obligation, responsibility, etc. Common term used in bankruptcy court to describe the process of eliminating debtor obligations.

Discounts: Selling Accounts Receivable or Bad Debts at an amount normally in excess of 51% of the outstanding balance.

Dispossession of property: Taking away property against the owner's wishes, normally as a result of non-payment.

Erroneous information: False, misleading or incorrect data. Frequently found in consumer medical or credit files across America.

Excessive inquiries: Term used by potential lenders when inspecting a credit report to indicate that the consumer has too many inquiries by other prospective creditors. This indicates that a consumer may be securing an unusually high amount of potential debt, even though there is no information line that explains whether a previous creditor/inquirer has actually extended credit to this consumer. Many consumers end up with these notations (unwittingly) when out shopping for new automobiles.

Exempt assets: Assets not at risk of being seized or forfeited as a result of legal action.

FADA: Federal Assets Disposition Association was created by the federal government during the Reagan administration to handle the sale of assets acquired from banks or savings and loans that have failed. Unfortunately, FADA was not successful in this quest and was closed/replaced by the Resolution Trust Corporation (RTC).

FDIC: Federal Depositors Insurance Corporation, operated/backed by the federal government to insure/guarantee the deposits of consumers in member banks. Normally depositors are insured against default/insolvency up to $100,000 per account.

Financial management: Technique used to balance income vs. expenses. Responsible financial management usually results in an excess of monies available as a result of this technique. (This style of managing finances has yet to be mastered by the United States Government.)

Flaky loans: Questionable loans made by banks in the 1980's such as student loans or land development loans. (See defaulted student loans.)

Fraudulent activities: Transactions designed to swindle consumers or creditors, normally cheating these groups out of goods, services or assets (also see "sign of the beast").

Freebie report: A copy of your credit report given to you at no charge for one of two reasons...every consumer gets a free report from TRW just for asking and every consumer gets a free copy of their credit report if they have been declined credit.

Frivolous and irrelevant: Term used by credit reporting bureaus when they suspect a consumer is trying to bombard them with letters disputing entries on their credit report. Credit bureaus can throw out disputes if they can justify their claim or suspect the intervention of a credit repair clinic.

Getting bulletproof: Term used to describe process to insulate a person from lawsuits, garnishments, creditor intrusion and harassment. Popularized in Texas during the late 1980s...now being utilized by consumers/ businesspeople in California and the east coast.

Greed: A motivating instinct shared by collections and credit managers that instills a desire to maximize amount of monies received. A major factor that inspires individuals to open collection agencies.

Handwritten correspondence: Technique used to question, inquire or dispute the validity of information lines contained on a credit bureau report. These letters are directed to the credit reporting agency that is spreading this erroneous/derogatory information in hope of eventual removal.

Hired gun: Term used to describe the hiring of third party debt collectors or attorneys to emotionally pummel a consumer in hopes of collecting an overdue account.

Hot checks: Drafts on a bank account that will be or have been returned by the bank for insufficient funds to pay face amount of check issued.

I.R.S. refund offset program: Effort initiated by the Department of Education to recover defaulted student loans by seizing the tax refunds of consumers with the assistance of the Internal Revenue Service.

Interrogatories: Sworn statements made in writing as a result of a list of questions/inquiries by attorneys in court (or post judgment) action.

Intimidation: Inspiring or inducing fear (a favorite tactic of debt collection agencies).

Inquiry line: A line at the bottom of a credit reporting indicating that a prospective lender has obtained a copy of your credit file with the possible intent of extending you credit.

K.I.S.S.: Keep It Simple Stupid; a philosophy that has re-emerged in the 1990's and encourages consumers/ businesspeople to make a point without a lot of bull. Straight-forward presentation of ideas or alternatives are more frequently met with a quicker and more positive result.

Knee Breaker Collection Agency: Generic name used to describe a collection agency that may use techniques that are not endorsed by the American Collectors Association or deemed legal by the federal government under the Fair Debt Collections Practices Act (also see Vito).

Lawyers: *See* Attorneys.

Malpractice litigation: Lawsuits filed by patients against medical caregivers for poor or injurious services performed/

received. Many times these suits are frivolous and without merit and are mere attacks by patients and their unscrupulous lawyers looking for a quick payoff from an insurance company.

Manual reporting: The act of having to physically verify/confirm credit or legal information for credit bureau reports. This process normally takes longer and due to volume of inquiries, results in non/late verification of information contained in credit reports.

Marketshare: Portion of a particular marketplace dominated by a company selling/rendering goods/services.

Negative remarks: Statements or grades assigned on credit reports due to late payment, non-payment or default on debts owed to creditors. Bankruptcies and liens also show up under this category.

Old and cold: Term used to describe tactic of removal of aged (normally negative) credit information lines from a credit report. Works on expectation of older files not being available for verification by creditor when requested by credit reporting agencies.

Old debts: Debts that have been charged off/written off by a creditor, normally referred to an outside "third party" collector. Old debts are usually those debts/accounts that have not had charge or payment activity for over 2 years and are the easiest to negotiate payment/removal from credit reports with creditors.

Open account: An account with a creditor that is still on the books and in the opinion of the original creditor, collectible. These types of accounts usually are reported/updated to the credit bureaus and report late payments and can be the most difficult to negotiate with a creditor.

Oxymoron: A term that contradicts itself, such as "jumbo shrimp" or "military intelligence" or "ethical debt collector" or "reasonable legal fee."

Phantom companies: Former banks or other lenders that have either gone bankrupt or been acquired, but their line of information still remains on a credit report. These are normally the easiest to remove from a credit report since the original creditor no longer exists and therefore cannot confirm an entry when requested by credit reporting bureau.

Positive identification: A means to identify without a doubt the identity of a consumer wishing to obtain a copy of their credit file. A check and balance designed to keep unauthorized people from gaining access to your information.

Postdated checks: A check with a date in the future, a technique utilized to commit a person to make payment after the date written on the check.

Pre-approved credit card: An offer, normally extended through the mail, to a consumer for a credit card without

offers are created through the screening efforts of credit grantors by purchasing mailing lists of consumers that fit into specific spending and payment patterns.

Profit & Loss Statement: A timely accounting function that shows a reconciliation of all gross income and expenses to offset the same, arriving at a net profit (or loss) figure.

Prospective creditor: A credit grantor that has not yet agreed to loan/lend monies for the purchase of a home or automobile, or through the issuance of a credit card.

Red ink: Term used to describe losses sustained by any financial entity. When individual consumers drown in red ink they may end up filing for bankruptcy; when the U.S. government engages in this financial activity it holds another treasury note or bond auction.

Red lined: A term popularized by many government agencies and banking institutions in the 1980s to single out a particular region of the country. Visualize a state or group of states on a map with a bold "red line" around their borders, indicating a negative lending posture.

Regulatory agencies: Any agency empowered by either local, state or federal authorities to enforce civil laws.

Reply card tracer: Used by Postal Service to track down return receipts that never returned to verify delivery of parcel.

Re-prioritize: The resetting of priorities in one's life, usually due to a dramatic change in circumstances.

Return receipts: Work in conjunction with Certified Mail, receipts (green card for domestic mails/pink card for international) give the sender a record of who actually received the letter or package sent.

Revolving charge card (or credit line): Commonly issued by major department stores and major banks, it requires a monthly payment sufficient to amortize the outstanding balance. Note/example: If consumers pay only the minimum balance on a $10,000 credit card and do not use the card for any additional purchases, it will take over 25 years to amortize/payoff the debt.

Risk free: A concept used in lending to describe the risk vs. return of certain types of consumer/business loans. Also refers to overdraft protection checking accounts at the House of Representatives bank in the 1980's.

Roll over: What many consumers do when dealing with credit bureaus or collection agencies, giving up without a fight. Also used to describe the apathy displayed by most Americans when asked about their input in the law making/enforcement process or budgetary responsibility of congress.

RTC: Resolution Trust Corporation formed by the federal government in the late 1980's to replace/bail out FADA in their quest to sell off assets acquired from failed banks and savings and loans.

Scams: Fraudulent plans or schemes designed to separate a consumer from their money without delivering on promised goods, services (training) or value.

Scoring system: A tool used by prospective lenders to grade the credit worthiness of a potential borrower.

Secured credit cards: A major national credit card (normally Visa or MasterCard) that has a credit limit secured by a cash deposit placed with the issuing bank by the card holder. A positive recovery step for consumers that have gotten into credit problems but need a credit card in order to get a hotel room, a rental car or other business/travel related activities.

Sign of the beast: A reference to Satan in a passage from the Revelations chapter of the Bible; also used as a derogatory term describing debt collectors and some attorneys.

Snake oil: A negative term used normally by an individual to discredit another. Refers to selling or promoting something that falsely claims inflated results or expectations. (A favorite term of the American Collectors Association, a trade group representing debt collectors across the U.S.)

Social security number: a nine digit number issued by the Health and Human Services Administration to identify

Americans for future social security benefits. This number has evolved into the years as a national identifier for Americans, a serial number now used for referencing credit information files, military and school records, etc.

Technical jargon: Terminology used to explain certain business or legal situations, many times confusing the individual making the inquiry. Frequently used by members of congress, the legal and medical professions and the credit reporting industry.

Threats: An indication or warning of probable trouble. (See debt collectors.)

Trial by fire: Term used by individuals that have acquired "street smarts" by dealing directly with problems as addressed by average consumers. These individuals frequently include graduates from the *school of hard knocks.*

Usual and customary: Insurance company term to describe fees for goods or services usually associated with the medical profession. Results from an average of current fees charged for a particular procedure performed by medical caregivers in a certain market area.

"Vito": Name used to describe any individual in the debt collection industry that may use techniques that are not endorsed by the American Collectors Association or deemed legal by the federal government under the Fair Debt Collections Practices Act.

Vocational schools: Non-traditional institutions of higher learning designed to train students in job skills as opposed to educational degree plans in specific areas of study. Vocational schools can graduate students in 6-24 month course studies as opposed to 48 months in traditional colleges/university programs.

Index

Bibliography

Abend, Jules. "Credit Matters: the Privacy Issue," **Stores Magazine** (February 1990), 18-19.

Applewhite, Ashton and others. **And I Quote.** New York: St. Martin's Press, 1992.

"Bankers, House to Clash Over Credit Reports," **The FDIC Watch** (March 29, 1993), 4.

Bartlett, John. **Familiar Quotations.** Boston, MA: Little, Brown and Company, 1980.

Belew, Joe. "Privacy and the Fair Credit Reporting Act," **Journal of Retail Banking** (Summer 1990), 60-64.

Bukro, Casey. "Field's Settles Claim it Violated Credit Act in Hiring," **Chicago Tribune** (May 14, 1993).

"Consumer Credit Reports Get Special Attention," **ABA Banking Journal** (March 1992), 7-8.

Corman, Linda. "Don't Change Privacy Law, Consumers in Survey Say," **American Banker** (June 12, 1990).

"Credit Bureaus Simplify Reports to Improve Accuracy," **Card News** (April 19, 1993).

Culligan, Joseph J. **You, Too, Can Find Anybody.** Miami, FL: Hallmark Press, 1993.

Davis, Kristin. "Credit Bureaus: Will They Get It Plight?" **Kiplinger's Personal Finance Magazine** (March 1992), 82-85.

Davis, Kristin. "Credit Errors: When They Just Won't Go Away," **Kiplinger's Personal Finance Magazine** (October 1991), 32 & 34.

Davis Kristin. "When the Credit Bureau Fouls Up." **Changing Times** (September 1990), 99-101.

Detweiler, Gerri. **The Ultimate Credit Handbook.** New York: Plume, 1993.

Dover, Benjamin F. ***BACK OFF!*** **The Definitive Guide To Stopping Collection Agency Harassment.** Fort Worth, TX: Equitable Media Services, 1994.

"Do you need credentials?" **Changing Times** (November 1990), 102.

French, Scott. **Credit: The Cuttting Edge.** Boulder, CO: Paladin Press, 1988.

Friedman, Jon and John Meehan. **House of Cards: Inside the Troubled Empire of America Express.** New York: Putnam, 1992.

Gallene, Denise. "Credit Firms Attempt to Clean Up Act," **Los Angeles Times** (May 18, 1993).

Garrett, Echo Montgomery. "Why You Still Can't Rely on Credit Bureaus," **Money Magazine** (March 1993), 17.

Garsson, Robert M. "Bill to Ease Correction of Credit Errors Is Called Harmful to Small Lenders," **American Bankers** (May 28, 1993).

Garsson, Robert M. "States Fight to Keep Credit-Data Powers," **American Banker** (August 3, 1992).

Gilgoff, Henry. "Forget It, Deadbeat; Credit reports now use plain English," **Newsday** (May 6, 1993), 45.

"Happy Holidays From TRW," **The National Law Journal** (January 11, 1993), 6.

Kantrow, Yvette D. "Credit Repair Firm Buying Bank to Issue Cards," **American Banker** (July 25, 1991), 6-7.

Kirby, Paul. "Legislation Introduced to Improve Accuracy of Credit Reports," **States News Service** (March 19, 1993).

Kurshan, Jerome. "Let's Curb Social Security Number's Uses," **New York Times** (April 5, 1993), editorial section, 16.

"Lawmakers Unveil 1993 Version of Fair Credit Reporting Legislation," **Banking Policy Report** (March 15, 1993), 2.

Lazzareschi, Carla. "Money Talk: Repairing the Damage of Student Loan Default," **Los Angeles Times** (May 2, 1993), business section, 4.

"Legislature Considering Credit Reporting Regs," **United Press International** (March 15, 1993).

Manners, John and Lani Luciano. "Keep Their Eyes Off Your Credit Data," **Money Magazine** (June 1991).

McNeil, Alex. **Total Television.** New York: Penguin Books, 1991.

Morrall, Katherine. "Credit Card Scoring: Profit by the Numbers." **Bankers Monthly** (November 1991), 25-29.

"New Horizons: Japanese Consumer Credit Reporting Is Taking on an American Flavor with TRW Information Systems and Services' Purchase of a 4% Stake in Central Communication Bureau, Japan's Fourth-Largest Credit Bureau," **CardFax** (March 22, 1993).

"Oops! The Town That Bounced," **People Magazine** (November 25, 1991) 164.

Pankau, Edmund J. **Check It Out.** Houston, TX: Cloak & Data Press, 1990.

Peter, Dr. Laurence J. **Peter's Quotations.** New York: Bantam Press, 1989.

Porsch Jr., Robert J. "Leave a Good Law Alone," **Direct Marketing** (June 1991), 66-68.

"Protect Your Privacy," **Changing Times** (October 1990), 96.

Riley, Michael G. "Sorry, Your Card Is No Good," **Time** (Apil 9, 1990). 62.

Rothfeder, Jeffrey. "Congress Should Put a Lid on What Credit Bureaus Let Out," **Business Week** (July 2, 1990). 57.

Rothfeder, Jeffrey. "For Sale: All Your Best Kept Secrets," **Sacramento Bee** (April 14, 1993), B7.

Rothfeder, Jeffrey. **Privacy For Sale.** New York: Simon & Schuster, 1992.

Schwartz, Evan I. and others. "Credit Bureaus: Consumers Are Stewing and Suing," **Business Week** (July 29, 1991), 69-70.

Schwartz, Evan I. "It's Time to Clean Up Credit Reporting," **Business Week** (May 18, 1992), 52.

Schwartz, Joe. "Privacy Fears," **American Demographics** (September 1991), 47.

Schwartz, John. "Consumer Enemy No. 1," **Newsweek** (October 28, 1991), 42 & 47.

Schwartz, Jon and Brad Edmondson. "Privacy Fears Affect Consumer Behavior," **American Demographics** (February 1991), 10-11.

"Senators Bryan, Bond Revise Earlier Fair Credit Reform Bill," **BNA's Banking Report** (April 12, 1993), 496.

Shaw, Stephen. "Inaccuracy, Fraud and Information Privacy," **Buffalo (NY) News** (May 16, 1993).

Siler, Charles. "A Credit Giant Charges Ahead: Pritzkers Push Trans Union into Canada, Europe," **Craines Chicago Business** (February 17, 1992),

Skousen, Mark. **Complete Guide to Financial Privacy.** Alexandria, VA: Alexandria House, 1982.

Slom, Stanley H. "Credit Changes: New Laws Could Hamper Check Acceptance," **Stores Magazine** (May 1992), 45,

Stern, Linda, "Rebuild Credit History with a Secured Card," **The Reuter Business Report** (April 21, 1993).

"Student Loan Defaulters Risk Losing Federal Tax Refunds," **U.S. Newswire** (April 15, 1993).

"TRW Issues Credit Reports San Gibberish," **Los Angeles Daily News** (April 26, 1993), business section, 6.

"TRW Listens to Consumers; Introduces 'Plain English' Credit Reports," **PR Newswire** (April 23, 1993).

"TRW To Pay Vermont Residents For Erroneous Tax Status Information," **Credit Risk Management Report** (January 4, 1993).

Wilcox, Ella Wheeler. Passage excerpted from "Protest," **Poems of Problems** (1914). As quoted in the Oliver Stone film "JFK", distributed by Warner Bros. (1991).

Woller, Barbara. "Don't Pay Someone to 'Fix' Your Credit," **Gannett News Service** (March 11, 1993).

Young, Jae-Bok. "Secured Credit Cards Post 21% Growth," **The Christian Science Monitor** (March 23, 1993), economy section, 9.

"Your Credit Rating," **Consumer Reports** (October 1990), 648.

Suggested Reading

Culligan, Joseph J. **You, Too, Can Find Anybody.**
Miami, FL: Hallmark Press, 1993.

Detweiler, Gerri. **The Ultimate Credit Handbook.** New
York: Plume, 1993.

Dover, Benjamin F. **Back Off! The Definitive Guide to
Stopping Collection Agency Harassment.** Fort Worth,
TX: Equitable Media Services, 1994.

Eisenson, Marc. **The Banker's Secret.** Elizaville, NY:
Good Advice Press, 1992.

Friedman, Jon and John Meehan. **House of Cards: Inside
the Troubled Empire of American Express.** New
York: Putnam, 1992.

Pankau, Edmund J. **Check It Out.** Houston, TX: Cloak &
Data Press, 1990.

Rothfeder, Jeffrey. **Privacy for Sale.** New York: Simon &
Schuster, 1992.

Skousen, Mark. **Complete Guide to Financial Privacy.**
Alexandria, VA: Alexandria House, 1982.

THE DOVER REPORT SURVEY

The request for current information and insights into consumer issues from our readers continues to grow, so tell us what you want to see in our upcoming newsletter!

Please rate on a scale of 1-10 (with 10 being most desirable) what information is most important to you:

_____ Credit reporting issues
_____ Debt collector problems
_____ Avoiding bankruptcy
_____ Family trusts
_____ Smart Banking
_____ Tax law changes and their impact
_____ Telemarketing scams of the month
_____ Automobile purchase/service issues
_____ Aggressive investment opportunities
_____ Money saving ideas
_____ Back child support collection ideas
_____ Protection of assets
_____ Investing for retirement
_____ Consumer deal of the month
_____ Finding people
_____ Other (please specify):

How often would you like to see the report published?
____**Monthly** ____**Quarterly** ____**Bi-annually** ____**Annually**

THE DOVER REPORT SURVEY
Equitable Media Services
Post Office Box 9822-DRS
Fort Worth, TX 76147-2822

Name:_____

Address:_____

City, State, Zip:_____

KNOWLEDGE IS POWER

❏ **YES!** I realize that the material covered in this book can be outdated due to changes in the credit reporting industry and want to be informed. Please add my name to your mailing list for any future information updates you may make available.

Name:_____

Address:_____

City, State, Zip:_____

Enclose this page (or a copy of) to:

Equitable Media Services
Post Office Box 9822-**NO BS**
Fort Worth, TX 76147-2822

or you may e-mail your name and address to Benjamin Dover at
CompuServe address: 75053,3635
Internet address: bendover@onramp.net

Equitable Media Services maintains the highest degree of privacy at all times and does not sell or disclose mailing list or client information to any outside/third party.

All correspondence is CONFIDENTIAL.

DID YOU BORROW
THIS COPY?

Order additional copies of *Life After Debt:* **The Blueprint For Surviving In America's Credit Society** by Benjamin F. Dover.

Please rush to me _____copies of *Life After Debt* I am enclosing **$21.00** per copy (*$16.95 plus $1.31 tax and 2.74 postage/handling*).

Name:_____

Address:_____

City, State, Zip:_____

Enclose this page (or a copy of) with your **check** or **money order** and mail to:

Life After Debt
Equitable Media Services
Post Office Box 9822-**NO BS**
Fort Worth, TX 76147-2822

❏ **YES!** Please add me to your mailing list for all future updates.

Equitable Media Services maintains the highest degree of privacy at all times and does not sell or disclose mailing list or client information to any outside/third party.

If you are interested in obtaining quantity discounts, please write to the address above for additional information.

All correspondence is CONFIDENTIAL.